The New Middle Ages

Series editor
Bonnie Wheeler
English & Medieval Studies
Southern Methodist University
Dallas, Texas, USA

The New Middle Ages is a series dedicated to pluridisciplinary studies of medieval cultures, with particular emphasis on recuperating women's history and on feminist and gender analyses. This peer-reviewed series includes both scholarly monographs and essay collections.

More information about this series at
http://www.palgrave.com/series/14239

Joel T. Rosenthal

Social Memory in Late Medieval England

Village Life and Proofs of Age

Joel T. Rosenthal
Department of History
Stony Brook University
Stony Brook, New York, USA

The New Middle Ages
ISBN 978-3-319-69699-7   ISBN 978-3-319-69700-0   (eBook)
https://doi.org/10.1007/978-3-319-69700-0

Library of Congress Control Number: 2017960341

Cover illustration: Mono Circles © John Rawsterne/patternhead.com

Printed on acid-free paper

This Palgrave Macmillan imprint is published by Springer Nature
The registered company is Springer International Publishing AG
The registered company address is: Gewerbestrasse 11, 6330 Cham, Switzerland

To the women of the villages: if only we could hear their memories

CONTENTS

Contents

CHAPTER 1

Introduction

Abstract The Proof of Age was a document produced at a hearing held by the escheator to determine whether the heir to property held in chief had reached legal age. The substance of the proceeding was the collection of 12 memories from men of the village telling how or why they remembered the date of the heir's birth and baptism 21 years ago (or 14, or 16, for heiresses). These memories open a window on the events of daily life: seeing the baptism, burying a relative, buying a horse, telling of a great windstorm, and more of such memories. Whether all the memories were based on "what really happened" or were formulaic responses, has been debated. But regardless, they were all deemed sufficient and in their large numbers they shed light on the ordinary life of ordinary men (and what these men learned from "their" women).

Keywords Social memory • Orality

Historians often use the metaphor of weaving a tapestry, or perhaps it is painting a mural. In these essays my goal is to create a mosaic, arranging thousands of small tesserae—mostly coming to us in the form of "one liners" of memory—so we can step back and admire a coherent picture of ordinary life, mostly at the village level, in late medieval England. The small units we have at hand to work with are the memories—the social

© The Author(s) 2018   1
J.T. Rosenthal, *Social Memory in Late Medieval England*, The New Middle Ages, https://doi.org/10.1007/978-3-319-69700-0_1

memories as offered by the 12 jurors at a Proof of Age proceeding—as we chart them across 75 years of life, death, and memory.

The literature on social memory is vast—far beyond the scope of this small volume to do more than to touch in passing—but what I offer below is based on the idea that what people claimed they remembered from around the time the heir was born and baptized—whether the memory given was "true" or fabricated for the occasion—reveals which events, interactions, life milestones, and personal affairs were pulled out as the critical mnemonic. Which memory to offer? Today, were we asked to peg an event, such as a birth or a marriage or a death, against some point in the 1990s, what would we choose to tie an individualized or personal memory to the central event, such as a baptism? The coincidence of the personal, the social, or sometimes the external, with that baptism (or whatever we are trying to pin down) would be our guide; socially credible, probably known to our peers, fitting into the context of community and local culture. Going back 21 years we would have to take into account the vagaries of time and the crowding of events, the uncertainties of personal recollection, and sometimes at least the need to choose. But against the currents of erosion and fading colors, there was, in the late medieval world of orality and the networking of friends and neighbors in the life of village or local community, a process of recovery, usually resting on the most prosaic of events and giving us a glimpse into the sort of experiences that held their own in men's memories over the years.

Proofs of Age are fascinating documents and most of the memories they relate can be organized around some common themes. Their strengths and weaknesses will be explored, along with insights they provide into both the conventional and the unusual: familiar and oft-repeated recollections of births in the juror's family or of falls and broken shins as against the memory of an earthquake or a miracle cure. The format of this series does not allow for a full bibliographical exposition of all that has been said about the Proofs, nor about social memory and orality. The brief references we offer here are merely a starting point into these complicated and intriguing issues.[1] But we work from the premise that all of the thousands of memories we have were offered in the presence of the juror's peers, often, in fact, coming in the form of a joint memory from a number of the men. Credibility in the context of village life and memory was always on the table, whether the events being recalled "really" happened or not. Accordingly, to some extent building our mosaic on these memories rests on an act of faith. But against any issues of veracity (let alone of probability) we must keep in mind that whatever memory was offered, it was always accepted as a sufficient; no juror was ever questioned beyond the formulaic "how do you remember," let alone being contradicted or rebutted. One spoke before one's peers, and in doing so, when the Proofs are put together and we focus on their sameness and the common themes that link so many of them, we have our mosaic with its splashes and patches of the colors from which life is constructed. Memories of birth, death, marriage, accidents, a pilgrimage to Canterbury, fires and floods, and more of these ordinary events are the bread-and-butter of life. As these memories are offered by men who have no other port of entry into the historical record, we can express our appreciation for what they recounted in their fleeting moment on center stage.

NOTES

1. For the Proofs, these references cover some of the basic treatments and the attached notes and bibliographies are a gateway to the whole question of the Proofs as a primary source: Sue Sheridan Walker, "Proof of Age of Heirs in Medieval England," *Mediaeval Studies* 35 (1973), 306–23: Joel T. Rosenthal, *Telling Tales: Sources and Narration in Late Medieval England* (University Park, PA: Penn State University Press, 2003), 1–62, 161–79: J. Bedell, "Memory and Proof of Age in England 1272–1327," *Past and Present* 162 (1999), 3–27: Matthew Holford, "'Testimony (to some extent fictitious)': Proofs of Age in the first half of the fifteenth century," *Historical Research* (2008), 1–25: W. D. Deller, "The Texture of Literacy in the Memories of Late Medieval Proof-of-Age Jurors," *Journal of Medieval History* 38/2 (2012), 1–15: W. S. Deller, "Proofs of Age 1246 to 1430: their Nature, Veracity and Use as Sources," in *The Later Medieval Inquisitions Post Mortem: Mapping the Medieval Countryside and Rural Society*, ed. Michael Hicks (Woodbridge: Boydell, 2016), 136–60. The literature on social memory and orality and literacy is so extensive that a reference to a few basic (or classic) items has to suffice: M. T. Clanchy, *From Memory to Written Record: England 1066–1307* (Oxford: Blackwell, 2nd ed., 1993): James Fentress and Chris Wickham, *Social Memory* (Oxford: Blackwell, 1992). There is a special issue on oral history, memory, and the written tradition: *Transactions of the Royal Historical Society* 6th series, 9 (1999).

CHAPTER 2

Proofs of Age: The What and the Why

Abstract The Proof of Age proceeding really began when the heir petitioned that he or she was now of age. The guardians were "warned" of the impending hearing and the 12 men of the village, diligently questioned about their memory, told why they knew the heir had been baptized 21 years ago. The memories are noteworthy for the weight they place on acts of writing that set the date, for an attention to details and specific information, and to the exclusion of the direct voices or memories of women. Jurors often joined in a common memory and, since they opened with a self-stated age, we get a cross section of the middle-aged and elderly men who would have represented the lore and social memory of the village.

Keywords Age • Coming of age • Juries • Literacy and memory • Escheator

A Proof of Age proceeding was a common, routinized, and *pro forma* exercise, presided over by the escheator of the county and designed to elicit a set of memories used to establish the age of an heir or heiress.[1] For us, these memories open a window on aspects of ordinary and everyday life in late medieval England. The purpose of the Proof was to determine whether the heir to an estate held in chief (or by knight service) had now come of legal age and was therefore entitled to claim his or her property. A Proof, both as a process and then as the record of that process, was

© The Author(s) 2018
J.T. Rosenthal, *Social Memory in Late Medieval England*, The New
Middle Ages, https://doi.org/10.1007/978-3-319-69700-0_2

composed of or compiled from 12 supportive memories, offered by the 12 men of the village summoned for the occasion and now harking back to how or why they remembered the critical date of the heir's birth and/or baptism—some 21 or 16 or 14 years ago.[2] They were free to tie in virtually any sort of memory to the date that was of importance regarding the dating of the heir's entry into the world, as we shall see. If the proceeding found in the heir's favor—and by the late Middle Ages it was virtually certain to do so—the guardian of the estate who had held it in wardship was now called upon to surrender control. This was invariably done, and almost always without any voiced objection—and even at times without any proper response—from the guardian or his (or her) representative.

As the records of these proceedings have been preserved among the public records and published in a calendared form—standardized and recorded to satisfy a legal as well as political, economic, and social purposes—the memories offered can be organized into a number of topics or subject-headings that facilitate our look at daily life.[3] As we analyze the procedure that led to the Proof, it began with a petition from the now-of-age heir, or someone acting on her or his behalf, sent to the chancery, saying in effect that "it is about time." Assuming there was merit to the petition, as there usually seems to have been, the chancery then instructed the escheator to "warn" the guardians of the estate of the upcoming hearing at which proof of legal age would be adduced. The guardians, or their representatives, were summoned, presumably so they could object to its findings. At its simplest the instructions to the escheator could combine several steps or stages of the process, as when he received a writ "to take the proof of his age (i.e., the heir's age) in the presence of Adam atte Wode, in whose wardship he is by the king's grant."[4] After these preliminary steps the escheator received a writ *de etate probanda* authorizing him to hold a Proof of Age, that is, to summon that jury of 12 adult men so they, chosen from among their fellows of village or town or community, could offer their memories to support the "fact" that the requisite number of years had passed between the "then" of the heir's birth and baptism and the "now" of the claim to be of age. In this whole business our 12 men actually serve in a dual role: jurors who collectively built the case on which the claim was verified and witnesses on whose testimony the case rested. However, there is no indication that this dual role ever caused a problem touching either the value of the memories or any issues about a possible conflict of interest.[5]

In the 12 volumes of *Inquisitions Post Mortem* that provide our material there were an impressive numbers of Proofs of Age: Table 2.1 shows both

Table 2.1 Numbers of Proofs of Age and their distribution by counties

County	Vol. 15	16	17	18	19	20	21	22	23	24	25	26	Total
Bedford	2	3	1	2		1	1			1			11
Berkshire	1				1	1					1	1	5
Bucks			1	1				2		2	1		7
Calais					1								1
Cambridge		1		4			1					1	7
Cornwall			1	1		1					1		4
Cumberland				2	2			1	1	1	3	2	12
Derbyshire	1	1		2			2		1	1	2	1	11
Devon	1	3			1	1	2	4	1	2	3	3	21
Dorset	1	2		1	3			1		1	1		10
Essex	2		1	2	3	1		8	1	4	2		24
Gloucestershire	2	3	4	1		1	4	2	4	1	1	1	24
Hampshire	4			3	2	2		1	2	3			17
Hereford & the Welsh March	2	3			2			2	3	1	2	2	17
Hertfordshire					1				1		2	1	5
Kent	1	3			2	1	1				1	1	10
Lancaster		1		1				2					4
Leicestershire	1			1						1			3
Lincolnshire			3	4	6		2	1	3	1		1	21
London		1	3	4	1	2		2		1		1	15
Middlesex								1	2	1	1	1	6
Newcastle										1	1	2	4
Norfolk	1	1		3	3	1	4		2	2		1	18
Northampton	2					1	2	1	2		2	1	11
Northumberland	2		1	1	7			1	2	1			15
Nottingham	1			1		1			1	1			5
Oxfordshire		1		1	1	1		1	1		1	1	8
Rutland	1							1			1		3
Salop	4		1	1	1				2		1		10
Somerset		1	2	2	1	3			1		1	1	12
Staffordshire	1	1				2	1	2	1				8
Suffolk					2	2		1	2		1		8
Surrey	2				1			2	1				6
Sussex	2	2	1		1			3	3				12
Westmorland										1			1
Wiltshire					2		1	2	2			1	8
Worcester		1	1	2		1		4					9
Warwickshire			1	4		2							7
York & Yorkshire	1		2	5	2		3	2	4	5	5	3	32
Totals	34	28	22	49	47	24	27	49	42	32	27	32	412[a]

[a]This number includes damaged documents when the county can be identified. If the damage is such that the county cannot be identified, the Proof has not been counted

their incidence and their geographical distribution across the realm (including a few urban hearings).[6] Clearly, a Proof of Age must have been one of those activities—an administrative procedure of the king's government and of the "feudal system"—that brought large and important matters into the purview of the local scene and that drew in and relied on the voice of participants, men who were almost always at a social level a good dip below that of the heirs whose interests were at now stake.[7] The latter (and we abandon the gendered wording: "heir" will cover male and female claimants to estates) were from the upper reaches of society, with peers of the realm at the top but even the more modest of those making a claim to an estate being of considerable substance.[8] Because estates held in chief were very much part of what we might think of as the *ancient regime*, it is not surprising that they continued to be of importance well after our last volume of *Inquistions*.[9] In looking at the 414 Proofs of Age we have between 1377 and 1447 we are clearly dealing with fairly big business, involving hundreds of royal officials at various levels, not to mention the thousands of jurors.[10] A Proof was a social ritual in collective memory and, given the ups and downs of survival and the importance of real property, it must have been a familiar and serious business. Table 2.1 shows its spread across the decades and across the realm.

In addition to the escheator himself there was his staff, including those men, sometimes named, who had been sent to carry that "warning" to the guardian. The escheator also brought along a recorder or a secretary, he being tasked with the vital role of setting the memories, offered orally and in the vernacular, into the Latin that would become the written record that preserved the findings. And though holding a Proof of Age was but one of the escheator's regular duties, we have seen that it was a fairly regular one that might well take him across the length and breadth of his county.

Seen as a series of steps or stages, we can dissect the process that produced a Proof and look at each one in a close-up fashion. Ironically, much of our interest in the Proofs rests on the fact that so many of the memories were so close to being *pro forma*, with the overwhelming majority of them falling into a few inclusive or broad categories of things remembered and now being offered to the escheator (and this compression or grouping of memories was no doubt sharpened by the modern editorial conventions of calendaring and translation). Moreover, the long-term similarity of jurors's memories is really what makes it possible to offer a reconstruction of "ordinary" life over three-quarters of a century. The gist of the memories

offered by jurors in the 1380s are much like those offered by their coun-
terparts in the 1440s, few signs of change in either society or in memory.
In the 400-plus Proofs we have scores and scores of memories of the juror
seeing the baptism of the heir, or of recalling births and deaths and marriages in his own family, or of telling of falls that resulted in broken shins,
and more of the like. Since the positive findings of a Proof really must have
been anticipated and were rarely contested, neither guardian nor heir
seems to have felt much need to bring out the sort of heavy artillery we
have in law suits that approached the lofty level of *Jarndyce v. Jarndyce*.
The pedestrian memories of the jurors, as most of them are, seemed to
suffice regardless of the size of the estate, the stature of the heir, the date
of the Proof, or the venue at which it was being held.

Regarding the Proofs of Age as a category of primary source, a few
general considerations about the culture they reveal. One striking charac-
teristic of many of the memories is the privileged position accorded to
memories that rested in some fashion or the other on written documents,
whether it was a primer or a Bible in which was recorded the record, the
date of the baptism or a written contract, or an indenture for a secular
transaction. In the former type of memory, it was often no more than having witnessed the act of writing—as in seeing the priest set down the date
of the heir's baptism in a service book or in referring to when a lease had
been signed—that seemed to give that memory an iron-clad quality. And
although the act of writing referred to was usually done by someone other
than the juror himself, he did occasionally offer that he had been the one
to set hand to paper (or parchment). The many memories that rested on
the recollection of having seen or having been told about a key date that
had been set down in writing, as well as the context of such a record, will
be covered below. But the incidence of such memories and the high regard
in which they seem to have been held—across the realm and across the
decades—support the idea that by the fourteenth century, at least among
the laity of middling status, we are well along a road taking us from a world
where orality still held sway to one where literacy was not only becoming
the common exchange but where it perhaps carried more weight.

In the course of all the memories of such data as a birthdate being set
to writing, the jurors show considerable sophistication about the various
service books they saw in the church. Basic service books like the missal,
psalter, and breviary were identified, assuming they were correctly named
in the Proofs. But a few more details that may not testify to a juror's
literacy—though the odds were in favor of this by the mid-fourteenth

century—but we have men who talked of the birth or baptismal date being set down in the table of contents of the psalter, or in the great missal (implying the church also had a lesser missal), and a martyrology. One birthday was recorded in the calendar of Elizabeth's great missal, arguing for lay ownership of the volume. There was the calendar of the psalter plus a book of benefactors (*mortilagium*), and a bible into which the date was written in English. In a memory that touched on the role of a monk, the date went into the chapter book of the abbey. One juror remembered that the vital information had been written in "a manual in the church, in the calendar listing the feast of St Agatha," a testimony to first-hand knowledge and probably to being an eye witness. With the "church Bible" and the table of contents of a psalter both mentioned by jurors, we have an impressive list of the sort of books available in parish churches, perhaps owned in some part by the laity, and certainly familiar to men who dressed their memories with specific information about the mysterious world that was created and preserved by the use of the quill on paper or parchment.

Another aspect of both the procedure and the Proof is the impressive attention given to precise information, to details of all sorts, and to numeracy.[11] Against stereotypes about the vagueness of medieval life and lore (whether oral or written), jurors' memories—albeit terse and for the most part fairly standardized (and repetitive)—are very frequently quite precise in their attention to detail. Given that the heir's age is often "proved" by what seems an assertion of existential or circular reasoning—barely reaching the level of a simple syllogism—we have an abundance of hard information. Escheators were readily convinced, we might say, and a juror could make the case with a memory along the lines of something seemingly invulnerable to external proof or logic as "Katherine his daughter was baptized on the same day, and she was 21 and more on 7 October last" or "in the week that she was born, William, his son, was born who is now 16 years of age and more."[12] To the escheator's obvious and oft-asked question of "how he remembers this after so long a lapse of time" the sort of answers just quoted were invariably deemed to be *good enough*. A *pro forma* procedure, rather than a world of hard-nosed inquiry, clearly lies behind a willingness to take something like "John Roger, 46 and more, knows [that Margaret is of age] because Alice his daughter is the same age as Margaret."[13] The routinized nature of the proceeding, built on the foundation of the common lore of the village, is borne out by such memories as that of the juror who "had a son John baptized in the church that day and knows by counting the years from that baptism."[14]

But the fallback on this sort of circular reasoning does not preclude the frequent inclusion in a Proof of lots of details, strange as this may seem. All sorts of details are included or inserted to an extent that often seems to go well beyond what was needed for the occasion, especially when we are getting a memory based on things the jurors might only have known at second or third hand (and they have no reservations about admitting to this). The names—and rarely anything short of both Christian name and surname—of all the parties involved or even referred to are invariably given; almost no memories just trail off as "a man from the village" or some such, except perhaps when the hanging of a stranger was the memory of the moment. A felon, or a rare reference to a servant, may have stopped short of proper identification, but this would only cover a score or so of memories out of the thousands in the record, and it was a sign of class distinction or community membership. The self-stated ages of the jurors, and with a considerable range between the youngest and the oldest, will be discussed below. The precise dates of birth and baptism, both for the heirs and for those with similar milestones in the juror's own family, are often spelled out (in secular or regnal years), and even a few references to the time of the day are to be found; it was 9:30 a.m. for a memorable set of events, and even earlier for the ceremony in church, the baptism having been conducted before 9 o'clock.[15] One juror was about as precise as one could ask for: the heir was "baptised there on 31 August 1392 about the hour of vespers."[16]

Business affairs that jogged a juror's memory often entailed such details as the date and duration of financial terms to a contract or a lease, or perhaps giving the number of livestock bought or sold or stolen or coming to grief while crossing a swollen river. While the accuracy of a memory may be in dispute, whatever jurors chose to say was said in a clear and precise fashion. Furthermore, except for a very small number of memories that refer to a miracle cure or the evil eye, there are no references to the supernatural, the mystical, or the deeply introspective. In their thousands, they tell the tale as it was—or at least as it might have been. As has been said in a different context, the jurors' memories bring "a resolutely human and mundane perspective on sacred events."[17]

A further note when considering the genus, Proofs. In reading jurors' memories it behooves us to pay homage to the women on whom so many of those male memories rely. The women of that world are almost completely voiceless—often seen, often referred to, never heard.[18] In substance, so many of the memories of the jurors centered on women's roles in society—women pregnant, women in labor and childbirth, new mothers, midwives, nurses, godmothers, village gossips, telling of the celebration when a new mother was being churched, women as prominent faces and voices in the crowd that saw the baby carried to or from church, and so on. There are the wives and sisters and daughters of our jurors, while the ranks of the godmothers often included women from the higher levels of society when the heir was sufficiently well-born. Nor does this list of roles take into account those women who had been guardians of the estates during the heirs' minority, let alone those female heirs indicated in Table 2.2. Here we have young women, now coming of age and claiming their estates (or having them claimed on their behalf) but, as we said, never appearing on the stage. There are over 400 Proofs in the pool: 342 male heirs, 92 female heirs. So women, in their multitudinous roles and identities, were absolutely vital for the vast mosaic of memory that we seek to construct,

Table 2.2 Jurors' memories: individualized or collective

Volume	Number of Proofs	12 separate memories	Joint memories (2 or more jurors)	Damaged Proofs	Male heirs	Female heirs
Vol. 15 1–7 R II	35	13	21	1	28	6
Vol.16 7–15 R II	31	5	16	2	22	11
Vol. 17 15–23 R II	23	9	11	3	18	5
Vol. 18 1–6 H IV	50	24	23	1	40	8
Vol. 19 7–14 H IV	52	26	22	3	42	7
Vol. 20 1–5 H V	24	8	12	4	19	5
Vol. 21 6–10 H V	30	17	16	4	26	4
Vol. 22 1–5 H VI	51	48	2	–	36	15
Vol. 23 6–10 H VI	52	47	2	2	43	9
Vol. 24 11–15 H VI	34	31	2	–	25	8
Vol. 25 16–20 H VI	31	28	2	2	22	9
Vol. 26 21–25 H VI	26	22	4	–	21	5

just as they were for village life and family life. Nevertheless, as far as the memories of our jurors stand as our building blocks (or tesserae), we only know the women of that world when *their* men chose to bring them in.

The Proofs reflect the class structure of their world: heirs to estates claiming what was theirs and enabled by a process whereby men of lesser status spoke on their behalf. There is no way to judge how much this up-down relationship, one about to be preserved into the next generation as the heir came of age, affected the memories offered. While village life was obviously under the gaze of the lord of the manor, the jurors were not mere villeins, nor, as their memories about secular business tell the tale, were they under the thumb of the landlord. Some jurors had been servants, and many ran the errands surrounding such public events as the baptism, but they seemed to give little evidence of a mnemonic gulf between a memory of a baptism in their own family and the baptism of the high-born infant at the center of the Proof. While some of the daily realities of class and hierarchy can be winkled out of the Proofs, much is destined to escape our analysis.

$*$ $*$ $*$

We now turn to the process, the first turns of the wheel that would conclude with the Proof. After the petition indicating that the heir now claimed to have reached the age of majority, we leave the main road for a quick look at some of the guardians who had held the estate during the minority. Like the genealogies of our heirs or the memories of the jurors, these data open a door on tales of mortality and on the tangled links that could enmesh family and the transmission of claims and perquisites. Some guardians are identified in a laconic (and adequate) fashion: "He is in wardship to Queen Joan who should be informed" (on 20 December 1419). A more complicated matter but not hard to explain: the guardian "held by knight service of the bishopric of Lincoln, lately *sede vacante* and thus taken into the king's hand."[19] One Proof takes us well beyond county borders, as the guardian and holder of the wardship had been the "said Robert, whose father held by knight service of the alien priory of Newent which is in the king's hands on account of the war with France."[20]

As we have noted, the escheator's first steps were to warn—which usually really just meant to notify—the guardians of the estate of what was about to happen. They—either in person or through a representative—were summoned, though non-appearance was often the case, the Proof rarely being more than a formality. The complexities of high politics could occasionally offer interesting variations on guardianship and wardship: "his lands being in the custody partly of John Bell of Boston and partly of the executors of John duke of Lancaster and Thomas earl of Kent: they should be warned."[21] Sometimes the escheator reported in his laconic fashion about carrying out his duties, turning to the keepers of the minor's estate when instructed to "inform them of the forthcoming Proof of Age."[22] The men on his staff and sent by the escheator to deliver the warning might be named, giving us a few more individuals to set alongside our otherwise-forgotten jurors for their brief moment on the stage. John Hore, Geoffrey Peny, Richard Dare, and John Bukke brought the message, though in this case the guardians "did not appear."[23] The men sent on this sort of errand were identified as "William Cokke servant of the escheator, and Thomas Sleford."[24] Perhaps these details were preserved to indicate that the escheator was not at fault for the numerous no-shows. Also, the names may also have been necessary for these men to get paid.

But we are usually assured that efforts were made to contact the guardians—part of the regular routine—though often to little purpose: "John ap Hary was warned but did not come or send anyone to speak for him," presumably knowing that the heir's claim was about to be validated. The escheator acted responsibly, though: "the said Amice could not be found in the escheator's bailiwick and accordingly could not be warned to attend."[25] Clearly, many guardians just accepted the inevitable, as when "Lewis Johan esquire and Alice, his wife, widow of Francis de Court, executors of the latter, did not come nor did anyone of theirs, although solemnly charged and forewarned."[26] Failure to appear might have been due to circumstances beyond the guardian's control, as was the case with John Fresthorp, granted custody of an heiress's lands by Henry V: "John Fresthorp died long before the date of the attached inquisition, for which reason it was not possible to inform him."[27]

The petition to launch a Proof of Age for the estate of a 14-year-old heiress would come from her newly married husband, he being the person with a legal identity and one who, no doubt, might seek to enhance the charms of his child-bride. It was a man's world, even if they were her estates, and for young Maud, her "legal majority [was] claimed by Richard Harewell," her husband. In this case she was all of 15, a year after the claim might have been put. And though few heirs waited, or were forced to wait, until they were well beyond the legal age to lay a claim, we have an heiress of 38 and a male heir of 40, among the few so far beyond the age of majority. In the former case, Margaret's estate was now "claimed by

Richard de Radclyf, Margaret's husband," despite the interval since she had turned 14 or 16. She had been born in August 1385 and the Proof was held on 12 July 1424. Most likely a tangled inheritance and some intervening deaths, though the record gives no indication of why she now emerged as the heir. In the case of our 40-year-old male heir, the genealogy points to a string of intermediate heirs no longer on the scene: Richard was "son of Thomas, son of Agnes, sister of Benet, father of Richard de Fulsham, kinsman and heir of Richard, who held in chief."[28]

Finally, having cleared the preliminary steps, we come to the heir's moment, though ironically these important parties never appear in person in a Proof. Rather, the Proofs are about other peoples' memories of the heirs, key figures but always to remain off stage. The Proofs open by tracing the genealogical path whereby the heirs lay their claims to their estates, though because the case was not *yet* officially proven in law, the word "claims" often sets the scene: "Thomas Scales, who claims to have been born and baptized"[29] The line of descent was often quite simple: "Regarding his inheritance as son of William who held lands and tenements of Henry V in chief by curtesy after the death of Margaret" [the heir's mother].[30] More complicated trails can also be followed, out of interest for the light they shed on how families waxed and waned, how lines of descent often ran through women, how two sisters might be covered in one Proof though they were a few years apart in age, and how younger brothers and sisters might step forward as those ahead of them in the queue left the scene. Sometimes it was quite complicated, though the king's officers were accustomed to sorting out genealogical tangles as part of an inquisition post mortem.[31] We can see this tortuous path in a Proof: "Regarding the inheritance (of Thomas Dyneley) as son of William son of Eleanor one of the sisters of Elizabeth late wife of Peter Melborn, and as one of Elizabeth's kin and heirs, Peter Melborn held the lands and tenements which Elizabeth held in chief, by curtesy of the inheritance of Thomas and of Elizabeth's other kinsman and heir William Frodesley alias Hondesacre, chevalier, son of Isabel, other sister of Elizabeth."[32]

*   *   *

Time to turn to the jurors and their memories, our basic material for examination. Though the escheator put 12 men on oath, sometimes the record seems to indicate that the first juror named might act as a *de facto* foreman and that many of the memories that follow play off his opening statement, there being a tendency for jurors to say they agree with what a previous juror had said. The obvious question—asked both by the escheator and by readers today—comes when this first juror is "asked how he remembers this after so long a lapse of time" And in response, in this particular case, our first juror—our would-be foreman—established his credibility by naming the three godparents (two godfathers, one godmother), by giving the date and place of the baptism, and perhaps also by indicating that his own memory was still fresh and poignant because date of the birth in question coincided with the death of his own daughter.[33]

Though questions have been raised about the veracity of the memories—a problem discussed below—there was certainly an effort, in the compilation of the testimonies and the charging of the jurors, to indicate that it was all the result of serious inquiry. Only a rare departure from the straightforward, as in the few stabs at crude humor in a memory: a drunken fall that led to an injury, or being locked in the church by mistake, or seeing the baby urinate in the font.[34] But overall, while the conclusion of the proceeding may not have been in doubt, the formality and solemnity of the process was never abandoned or taken lightly. The gathering of the memories was *not* a casual matter. Whatever their faults as "real" memories, the record often carries a heavy emphasis on the search for true memory and for the need to follow proper procedure in collecting those memories. Even in a world of powerful memories and orality, rather than of written records, 21 years could be a goodly stretch and explicit statements about the *how* and *why* of memory did not go amiss. That the jurors could remember that far back was worth asserting, as well as that they often were in accord with the first juror's memory or that of the juror who had preceded them in giving his statement: "the other jurors, separately examined, agree and say that they know for the following reasons, all referring to events that happened 21 years ago."[35] The jurors had been "carefully examined," and again we come up against the common lore of the village: "the age of the said Robert is generally recognized in the parish of his birth." The Proofs are often given bite by such touches as "it was commonly said" or "it was common talk" or even that the jurors were unanimous.[36] A still stronger version of this assertion of careful probing and of an assurance of reliability makes the record: "it is well known throughout the parish that the heir is of that age … (and) all the parishioners … as well as his godfathers, neighbours, and friends, have carefully reckoned his age." Or it might be that "the jurors are unanimous that Henry Threlkeld is aged 21 years and more." In what is perhaps the most convincing coda of all, we are told that "the jurors had other notable evidence if it were necessary to produce it."[37]

These statements speak to the idea of common knowledge in the village or community about something as important as the birth of the heir. We are talking here about the emergence of the next lord or lady of the manor, a matter of considerable concern and an event the timing of which was apt to be well-noted and well-remembered. As we shall see from memories explored below, the time of the baby's birth and baptism would have been a time ceremony, of lavish eating and drinking, of gift-giving, and perhaps the occasion on which high-born strangers came from afar to name the baby, distribute largess, and leave a lasting memory of the occasion. Local men had probably been recruited to help decorate the church and assemble the "props," and memories of aristocratic godparents were likely to remain high points of village lore and reminiscences. Years later the first juror was still pleased to offer, in the Proof for the FitzWalter heir in 1423, that "the godparents had been Geoffrey, abbot of St. John's Colchester, John Burnham then prior of little Dunmow, and Eleanor, now wife of Edmund Bensted, knight."[38] The names of these worthies still came to mind, still fresh in memory, and this Proof hardly gives us the most impressive example of name-dropping in the Proofs. Thinking back to the baptism of a Moubray heir, one juror told of having seen "John, lord Say, lieutenant of Calais and god-father, give John a gilded sword."[39] And for a "can you top this," the juror who told of having seen Henry V lift the baby from the font would get blue ribbon.[40]

A total of over 400 Proofs of Age means, at full count, almost 5000 jurors (though partially damaged documents give us some relief). While the escheator needed 12 memories to bring for closure, it was not necessary to have 12 separate memories (though each memory had to have a juror's name attached to it). In many Proofs there is a reliance on a common memory, offered by a number of jurors speaking in agreement with each other and having their statements condensed in the record as one shared memory. Table 2.2 shows the incidence of this reliance on common or collective memories. This acceptance of the "buddy system" sheds light on the high level of networking we would expect within the village; communal activity, and shared memories of activity, coming from men of roughly equal status and often looped together over much of their lives by marriage, family, and/or long familiarity. These common memories are a good example of what has been referred to as "lifelong mutual familiarities" and later we will look at memories of marriage or death where the sister of one juror might have been the wife of another.[41] If men of the village were intertwined and networked when they offered a memory for a Proof, the odds are that comparable ties between them had been in existence 21 years ago.[42]

Joint memories were evidently as good as a string of 12 separate ones and the mini-groupings gave their testimony in any number of different arrangements and permutations. The men on a jury that only numbered ten for some reason could offer memories in groupings of two, three, two, and three jurors, or (for a full panel of 12) of four, four, and four. Any given Proof could combine single and joint memories; four men testifying separately, then five men in agreement on a single memory, and then two more, now speaking as one. The ages of those bracketed together were usually close, a logical result of shared experiences and perhaps of reminding each other of some common activity. We might have a group of three jurors (all over 45), then another of three (all 66), then of two jurors (both 60), then two more (45), and finally two together but a bit more disparate in age: 52 and 61. In a Proof with two groups of six men in each of the two memories offered, the first six in a common memory are aged 53, x (damaged text), 60, 57, 62, and 59; in the second group, it was x, 56, 57, 52, 59, and 58. A little disparity, perhaps, but no coupling the common memories of the 40-year-olds with men in their 70s.[43] It caused no problems when six jurors said, when their turn came, that all six "agree in all respects with the other jurors," while in a Proof where all 12 spoke to one memory, the assurance that all were 50 years and more may have lent an air of *gravitas*.[44]

When the men of the village were lined up for their special moment, they began with a recitation of their names and ages. That the jurors all had to be of sufficient years to have been at or beyond the age of majority 21 years ago (or only 14 or 16 for heiresses) would be an obvious *sine quo non*. And though a few suspicious cases can be found—a man who seemed too young or too old for the memory he offered—the ages given usually are in keeping with the match of age and experience, with progress through the life cycle. In demographic terms, the self-stated ages tilt us toward a pool of jurors of middle age, as we might expect, though we have a fair incidence of the elderly, they perhaps being the village elders and the keepers (and guardians) of the collective social memory. But, as we argue regarding the credibility of the memories, what jurors said about self-declared age had to be reasonable and appropriate. They stated their age in the company of their peers and that alone would surely have been a check on too much deviation (in either direction). We are hearing of ages from men often of a cohort that had grown up together, that had married and become fathers at roughly similar ages, and who went on to become the village elders if they lasted long enough. Though the ages of the jurors were probably rounded off in many cases, they also can be quite widely spread within a single Proof. Sometimes the knot was cut by the assertion or assurance that all the men "are aged 46 and more years."[45] And if a Proof in which every juror was 70 or more looks a bit peculiar, we also note that an occasional juror claimed to be in his 80s and one even is listed as being 89.[46] In a Proof from Wymbyssh, Wiltshire, 19 October 1428, the men are self-stated as being 80, 70, 71, 75, 84, 77, 70, 72, 73, 78, 76, and 74, and however far these advanced ages would seem to be from reality, the escheator and the other villagers must have found them acceptable. In another one of those few Proofs that do not follow the standard model of presentation, ages were given as they had been "then," rather than "now": 21 years ago, the Proof says, the jurors had been 16, 17, 26, 20, 20, 22, 16, 16, and 24 (in September 1380—as against their current age in October 1412). But taking into account the odd wrinkle, details were part of the whole business and jurors' ages—even though self-reported— are but more grist for the mills of numeracy and precise information.[47]

One of the mysteries surrounding the Proofs is the basis on which the 12 jurors were selected. Did the escheator pick and choose, or did some men volunteer, or was there a consensus regarding the long-time residents, or did the village "headman" point the finger? Though there is no way to answer this, it does not seem that age, per se, whether tilted toward the younger men or the elderly, was the key factor, as the mix of self-stated ages on so many juries indicates. But did younger men carry more weight when the Proof was that of a woman (an "heiress"), given that only 14 or 16 years, rather than 21, had passed since her baptism? Table 2.3, based on a limited sample, seems to say that while there might have been a tilt in this direction, it was more a tendency than a regular policy or practice. For the women, jurors in their 40s were to be found in greater numbers than for the whole pool as shown in Table 2.2, but not in any overwhelming fashion. This shift seems logical, given the shorter interval between baptism and the Proof. It may be enough to nudge us toward the idea that, however the 12 men were chosen, there was some recognition of the gap in years between the coming of age of male and female heirs. However, at best, this seems to have been just one of the factors that governed the choice of the 12 men who were called upon to give the escheator his jury.

Table 2.3 Age of jurors in Proofs of female heirs (drawn from two volumes of the IPMs

Volumes of IPM	Number of Proofs	Jurors in their 1930s	1940s	1950s	1960s	1970s	Total	Average[a]
Vol. 18	9	4	34	26	20	1	85	50.4
		5%	40%	31%	24%	1%		
Vol. 23	7	2	42	20	14	–	78	45.4
		3%	54%	26%	18%			
Total	16	6	76	46	34	1	163	
		4%	47%	28%	21%	1%		

[a]This "average" was compiled by averaging the separate Proofs and then computing an average of these averages. It is only meant as a rough guide

   In terms of the social dynamic of the Proof and the jurors' memories now being retrieved or generated, there is the occasional proof in which a "theme" or a line of related common memories dominates a good number of the statements. Whether the escheator tilted memories in this direction, saying he perhaps would be receptive to such kind of memories, or whether one man's memory just jogged his fellows into a similar vein of recollection, is a question we cannot answer. In one such Proof the theme was gifts to the new mother and five of the jurors followed this line: the gifts were of 12 partridges, 6 pheasants, 8 capons, 4 fat geese, and "a barren (*sterilem*) doe," as five jurors looked back in time. Another Proof ran along a similar vein, it again being that of meat and gifting: 12 partridges, two deer killed with the aid of two white greyhounds, two swans, a wild boar killed by the juror, and a present of 12 capons and 24 hens (*pulcrones*) (Table 2.4).[48]
   A study of the Proofs must take into account some of the numerous criticisms that have been levied against them regarding their reliability as guides to "real" events. Often coming from reviewers of the volumes of the *Inquisitions Post Mortem,* in which the Proofs appear, a critical finger is pointed at the repetitive use of certain memories and at the occasional duplication or near-duplication of a whole set of recollections as offered in proceedings well separated by time or place.[49] There is obviously some merit to these adverse views and one can wonder if the escheator sometimes arrived with the medieval equivalent of 3 × 5 inch note cards with types of acceptable memories, he being ready to hand them out to jurors who could not recall an event from the critical year. It has also been

Table 2.4   Jurors' self-stated ages

Volume of IPM	40–44	45–49	50–54	55–59	60+	Total
Vol. 15	74	62	100	33	42	311
1–7 RII	(24%)	(18%)	(32%)	(11%)	(13%)	
Vol. 18	80	75	129	61	83	428
1–6 HIV	(19%)	(18%)	(30%)	(14%)	(19%)	
Vol. 21	46	63	53	31	62	255
6–10 HV	(18%)	(28%)	(20%)	(12%)	(24%)	
Vol. 24	18	76	87	59	84	324
11–15 HVI	(6%)	(21%)	(27%)	(18%)	(26%)	
	218	276	369	182	271	1316
	(17%)	(21%)	(28%)	(14%)	(21%)	

suggested that the men of the village might consult among themselves until they found a fellow who did have a genuine memory—or at least a credible one—then to be "borrowed" for the occasion by the juror who was called to offer testimony.[50] It may not have been that easy to recall an event of precisely 21 (or 14, or 16) years ago and an "it was about that time, more or less" might be a better guide to some of the memories, though this could not be said to the escheator. One had to sound certain, to speak with precision and conviction. That the findings of a Proof were almost never brought into question by our day may have allowed—and perhaps occasionally encouraged—a rather slipshod search for a true memory.[51] And while in most memories the coincidence of timing between birth and baptism and the event remembered by the juror brought them very close together, now and then a juror spoke of something that he recalled from within the season or even the year of the critical time. Of course, the nature of the memory was a factor in this kind of timing: seeing the baptism in contrast to being called to defend the Scottish border.

Though the records never reveal their secrets, it is not hard to imagine an escheator arriving in the village, now in need of 12 circumstantial and convincing memories. But faced with the obstacle of 21 years into the past, he might well have pointed to the critical year and asked among the village worthies for someone who could come up with a memory of the baptism, who had a life-cycle event in his own family that year, who had been involved in a memorable bit of business, and perhaps who had done something really out of the usual: pilgrimage, or service for the king, or for one of the great nobles, or falling off a roof? Or it might be who had a document, or remembered seeing an act of writing. And once one man came up with something, we can picture him reminding his friends that they had shared the experience: fighting a fire, collecting props for the church for the baptism, being given a glass of wine from a proud father.

If the arguments cannot be resolved, it would seem that the best guiding wisdom to fall back on about the value and veracity of the Proofs is to accept that all the memories we have are *appropriate* ones for the occasion—offered as credible even if fudged in terms of reality and experience.[52] As social memory, these memories had to pass the test of collegial-credibility, consonant with local and village life, memories of events of many kinds, and not out of step with local mores. A man well known to have never left the village was not likely to stand up before his peers and offer a memory about his Jerusalem pilgrimage. The village tradesman in Somerset would scarcely peg his memory on a tale of military service along the northern border of the realm. Birth and marriages and deaths, as we shall see below, were public affairs; ritualized, sanctified, performed in public and frequently in the presence of and often with the involvement of other jurors—and were therefore familiar events to one's fellow jurors, and, no doubt, to many others in the village as well. Jurors always offered a memory of something *that could have happened*, whether it did or not.

Furthermore, scholars who have paid attention to the Proofs of Age acknowledge, whether they stand among the critics or the friends, that the documents offer glimpses of pedestrian activity, of "everyday life" that are otherwise hard to come by.[53] Men at the social level of the jurors rarely make a mark in the historical record and we are catching them now, even though they remain as little more than names, as they step forward for their moment on center stage. As we have said, the memories are detailed and precise, showing a special veneration for the written word and linked to the material world with a matter-of-fact air in offering what is usually a fairly prosaic tale. As the jurors lined up to offer their terse accounts of mnemonic events, they remind us of precocious children being called upon to step forward to recite Wordsworth's "Daffodils" and then being told to sit down so others could have their moment. Memories were both personal and social. They give us a brief glimpse of individual and private lives and they also set our jurors into a social context, a world of memories of matters done with and/or affecting family and companions, of the sacraments and the parish church, of business of many kinds, of love-days and of accidents, and—for better or for worse as the wheel was to turn—of birth and baptism, of life, and of death.

NOTES

1. For the escheator, E.R. Stevenson, "The Escheator," in *The English Government at Work: II. Fiscal Administration*, ed., William A. Morris and Joseph R. Strayer (Cambridge, MA, 19747), 109–67. For legal age, Frederick Pollock and Frederick William Maitland, *History of English Law* (rev. ed., S. F. C. Milson: Cambridge: Cambridge University Press 1968), II, 639–40. For the social rather than the legal, B. Gregory Bailey *et al.*, "Coming of Age and Family in Medieval England," *Journal of Family History* 33/1 (2008), 41–60.

2. A good scattering of heirs were beyond legal age when they moved to come into their own: "she was 19 years on 24 March last" (22/231); "the said heir was 27 years and more on the feast of the invention of the holy Cross last" (16/107), among many such examples. (For the full reference to vols. 22 and 16, note 3.)

   The 12 volumes of *Inquisitions* used in these essays run from vol. 15 to vol. 26. J. L. Kirby, ed., *Calendar of Inquisitions Post Mortem, vol. xv (1–7 Richard)*. (London, HMSO, 1970). (Kirby also edited volumes 16–20): *Calendar of Inquisitions Post Mortem, vol. xvi (7–15 Richard II)* (HMSO, 1974): *Calendar of Inquisitions Post Mortem, vol. xvii (15–23 Richard II)* (HMSO, 1988): *Calendar of Inquisitions Post Mortem, vol. xviii, 1–6 Henry IV (1399–1405)* HMSO, 1987: *Calendar of Inquisitions Post Mortem xix (7–14 Henry IV)* HMSO, 1992: *Calendar of Inquisitions Post Mortem, vol. xx, 1–5 Henry V (1413–1418)* London HMSO, 1995: J. L. Kirby and Janet A. Stevenson, eds., *Calendar of Inquisitions Post Mortem vol. xxi (6–10 Henry V)* (London, PRO, and Woodbridge, Boydell, 2002): Kate Parkin, ed., *Calendar of Inquisitions Post Mortem, vol. xxii (1–5 Henry VI) (1422–27)* (London: NA and PRO and Boydell, 2003): Claire Noble, ed., *Calendar of Inquisitions Post Mortem, vol. xxiii (6–10 Henry VI) (1427–1432):* NA and Boydell, 2004: M. L. Holford, S. A. Mileson, C. B. Noble, and Kate Parkin, eds., *Calendar of Inquisitions Post Mortem, vol. xxiv (11–15 Henry VI) (1432–1437)* NA and Boydell, 2010: Claire Noble, ed., *Calendar of Inquisitions Post Mortem, vol. xxv 16–20 Henry VI (1437–1442)* NA and Boydell, 2009: M. L. Holford, ed., *Calendar of Inquisitions Post Mortem, vol. xxvi (21–25 Henry VI) (1442–1447)* NA and Boydell, 2009. All references below to the *Inquisitions* are to volume number and item number within the volume.

3. 17/1110. Competing jurisdictions could make for a cumbersome proceeding: "To the chancellor of the county Palatine of Lancaster ordering

him to command the escheator to act according to an accompanying writ and to return the proof to the chancery of England" (22/356).

4. Charles Donahue, Jr., "Proof by Witnesses in the Church Courts of Medieval England: An Imperfect Reception of Learned Law," in *On the Laws and Customs of England: Essays in Honor of Samuel E. Thorne,"* el., Morris S. Arnold, Thomas A. Green, Sally A Scully, and Stephen D White (Chapel Hill, N. C., University of North Caroline Press, 1981), 127–158.

5. Helena M. Chew, "The Office of Escheator in the City of London during the Middle Ages," *English Historical Review,* 58 (1943), 319–30, explaining the paucity of urban Proofs of Age.

6. In contrast to many of the godparents, the jurors were usually of middling status, though I believe that they were of more respectable status than they are often thought to be. This slight revisionism will be explored below, especially on the context of their business activities and experience with long distance pilgrimage.

7. Obviously, peerage families figure prominently among the heirs: 19/665 for Anne, daughter of Lord Bardolf and wife of Sir William Clifford; 19/336 for John Moubray, earl marshal, to cite but two of many examples.

8. Margaret McGlynne, "Memory, Orality, and Life Records: Proofs of Age in Tudor England," *Sixteenth Century Journal,* 40/3 (2009), 679–97. McGlynne tallies the Proofs for both earlier and later days: in the reign of Edward I there are records of 35 Proofs, 30 for Edward II, 150 for Edward III. Looking at the Tudors, the numbers are 40 for the reign of Henry VIII, 56 for the years 1553–1603.

9. For the escheator notice to serve the writ of *de aetate probanda* was but one of his duties. M. S Giuseppi, *A guide to Manuscripts in the Public Record Office,* (2 vols., London, 1928), on the various writes used by chancery. The escheator reported to and worked for the exchequer as well as for the chancery.

10. Keith Thomas, "Numeracy in Early Modern England," *Transactions of the Royal Historical Society,"* 5th series, 37 (1987), 103–32.

11. 23/144: Another of this sort (23/307) "he married Joan ... on the day that John Benton was born and baptized and 21 years have passed since then."

12. 23/415.

13. 18/990: 23/144.

14. 18/667. For a look at a contemporary concern for the time of day, J. T. Rosenthal, "A Time to Read and a Time to Write: Dates, Days, and Saints in the Paston Letters," *Journal of the Early Book Society,* 16 (2013), 171–91. The memorable event of 9:30 a.m. offered as the juror's memory was that he had been at a swanimote where he saw a forester shoot a dog and then "hang it from the ranch of an oak called 'Ryggewith'" (21/876).

15. 20/130.
16. Troy Thomas, *Caravaggio and the Creation of Modernity* (London: Reakion books, 20216), p. 10.
17. The memories abound in hearsay material that jurors picked up, mostly from their own wives, but also in talking to the midwives and wet nurses and other women of the village, showing that conversation across gender lines clearly was socially permissible. A memory of hearing a woman cry out in labor hardly gives her much agency for her articulation, though there are a number of such memories (25/129). For a memory that seems both mysterious and demeaning, a juror "knows [the date of the baptism] because Margery his wife cried like an owl (*tutubavit*) and broke her right shin while going ... to see John baptised" (24/5650).
18. 21/216, 23/414, 15/658.
19. 16/75: the Proof was dated the Monday after St Martin, 7 Richard II, looking back to a baptism on the Thursday after All Saints, 35 Edward III.
20. 18/886.
21. 20/129: 23/314.
22. 25/294. Here we have a brief dialogue: "have William and Thomas [been] informed of the forthcoming proof of age ... they did not come, nor any on their behalf."
23. 19/475. The warning could be quite precise: "warned to be at Downham Market on 20 September, 1409," a message delivered by four men (19/608).
24. 20/129, 20/263, 16/340.
25. 22/230.
26. 22/882. This is another case of the husband claiming his wife's majority.
27. 22/365, for Margaret, 20/842 for Richard. In his case, the jurors—presumably older as memory ran farther back, are self-identified as being 63, 62, 65, 64, 63, 67, 66, 67, 68, 63, and 66. They could all have been in a modern day primary school at the same time.
28. 21/260.
29. 23/313.
30. On tracing relationships to determine the heirs, J. T. Rosenthal, *Patriarchy and Families of Privilege* (Philadelphia, 1991), 31–57; Michael Hicks, ed., *The Fifteenth-Century Inquisitions Post Mortem: A Companion* (Woodbridge: Boydell, 2012), and Hicks, ed., *The Later Medieval Inquisitions Post Mortem: Mapping the Medieval Countryside and rural Society* (Woodbridge: Boydell, 2016).
31. 22/674: "John kinsman and one of the heirs of Nicholas de la Beche. Namely, son of Margery Duyn, daughter of Isobel, Fitz Elys, daughter and one of the heirs of John de la Beche, elder, brother of the said Nicholas" (15/568).

32. 16/1053: 22/189.
33. For jurors who fell asleep—probably drunk—and got locked in the church, 19/999. This sounds like a standard item of village humor, and if a man told it about himself, as he does here, the risible must have outweighed the embarrassing, at least with the passing of the years.
34. 21/189.
35. 24/399: 18/1179: 21/368. There may have been some sharp questioning regarding the responses to "how, after so long a time" regarding memories.
36. 18/309: 15/891: 21/368: 16/336: 19/901: much the same, 19/997.
37. 22/189.
38. 19/336.
39. 24/566.
40. Paul Connerton, *How Societies Remember* (Cambridge, Cambridge University Press, 1989), p. 17. The whole passage seems to apply: "Village gossip is composed of this daily recounting combined with lifelong mutual familiarities. By this means a village informally constructs a continuous communal history of itself: a history in which everybody portrays, in which everybody is portrayed and in which the act of portrayal never stops. This leaves little if any space for the presentation of the self in everyday life because, to such a large degree, individuals remember in common."
41. In this regard, as Table II enlightens us one of the few changes over time is the diminishing number of joint memories by the 1440s, compared with the late fourteenth century.
42. 23/137; 21/368; 19/102; 20/130; 15/158.
43. 16/107: 15/658.
44. 25/128: in 17/148, all 12 "are 50 years and more."
45. 16/947. He remembered "because Robert his brother married his wife Joan ... on the same Monday." Since it was a female heir, born only 14 and a half years ago, the juror would have been about 75. Presumably, this was not a first marriage for Robert and Joan.
46. 20/720: 16/947. One juror tells of having ridden with the heiresses's great-grandmother (24/720). For a general discussion of old age and the role of the aged, J. T. Rosenthal, *Old Age in Late Medieval England* (Philadelphia: University of Pennsylvania Press 1996).
47. 26/351, and all taking place in the village of Herron, Essex, which seems suggestive in this context: 18/979. Also, 25/298.
48. The literature is briefly summarized in the Introduction, above.
49. E. Gillett, "Proofs of age," *the Amateur Historian*, Autumn 1962 (5/1961-63), 224-30 for the suggestion that jurors may have "borrowed" memories from their fellows.
50. For some Proofs with obvious flaws: 18/666, 18/309, 18/670, 19/478, and 15/652.

51. The suggestion about "appropriate" memories is offered by L. Beverly Smith, "Proofs of Age in Medieval Wales," *Bulletin of the Board of Celtic Studies*, 38 (1991), 134–44.

52. Christine Carpenter's assessment of the value of the Proofs—regardless of where one stands concerning their literal accuracy—is much in line with other have said: "The anecdotes offered by jurors to establish their memories of the child's birth or baptism are wonderful vignettes of the minutiae of ordinary lives, quite often of the lives of people about whom we would normally know nothings on this scale" (22/p. 33) from her general introduction to the five most recently published volumes of the *Inquisitions*.

CHAPTER 3

The Theater of Baptism

Abstract Dating the timing of the heir's baptism was the zero point of juror's memories and more memories related to this, in its many aspects and chapters, than to any other event. As the memories unroll the tale, the whole story of baptism embraces memories about fetching the midwife and the godparents and the wet nurse and sometimes even the priest. The church had to be prepared, the various players assembled and a range of props made ready, and the ceremony itself—a public event for the villagers—performed. This could go smoothly and many jurors had been spectators; others had played various roles that they were still happy to talk about. After the baptism had been performed there were memories from and about men who had carried the good news, often in return for a handsome reward, and finally—to close the drama—we have memories of the feast with accompanying gifts held to celebrate the churching of the mother and her return to society.

Keywords Midwives • Wet nurses • Godparents • Ritual and ceremony

Jurors' memories of the baptism of the heir stand in dead center of our concentric circles of recollection and testimony. Moreover, it was more apt to be the baptism, rather than the birth itself—or the two linked as one memory—that loomed so large and so vital in the memories offered.

© The Author(s) 2018   29
J.T. Rosenthal, *Social Memory in Late Medieval England,* The New
Middle Ages, https://doi.org/10.1007/978-3-319-69700-0_3

After all, the birth of the child in question was women's business—private business—and therefore it made less impression on the jurors who, except for a few odd memories that are ambiguous in their phrasing about a male presence at the birth, would only know of childbed and birthing at secondhand or even at some farther remove. Women's labor and the baby's birth took place behind closed doors, whereas the public ceremony of the baptism was held in the parish church, the spiritual and probably the physical and social center of the village or the community. Furthermore, it was the sacrament of baptism that cleansed the newborn child of the impurity that rested on the manner of its conception, let alone on her or his descent from Eve and Adam. It was that baptism that now prepared the child for entry into the community of Christ and Christendom. The Proofs offer hundreds of memories circling around the various aspects of the ceremony and these can be roughly divided into two large categories. The first are the memories—the subject of this chapter—that refer to the baptism of the heir who is now about to come of age. The second are the many memories of birth and baptism in the juror's own family; these will be dealt with in Chap. 4 on village life.

Though none of our parishioners and probably very few of their parish priests were likely to know the actual wording of a recent declaration about the need for and power or efficacy of baptism as enunciated by Pope Eugenius IV, the papal authority and the strength of local custom and lore converged regarding this first sacrament: "Holy baptism holds the first place among all the sacraments because it is the gate of spiritual life; for by it we are made members of Christ and of the body of the Church ... the efficacy of this sacrament is the remission of all sin, original sin, and actual, and of all penalties incurred through this guilt." Jurors' memories indicate that their thoughts ran along the same lines, though in their statements to the escheator they were wont to express themselves a good bit more concisely than did the vicar of Christ. One juror summed up the many stages of the ritual—what we divide into the numerous acts and scenes of a drama—by labeling them as simply "the act of baptism."[1] Jurors could be quite explicit about affirming the official view of the need for and efficacy of baptism—of how, through baptism, the infant became a member of the body of believers. The child was now eligible to receive the blessings that stemmed from Christ's sacrifice as it was known to the laity through the rituals and teachings of his church. As one juror offered his memory, he had "met many men and women coming from church who told him that Walter was baptized and a Christian."[2]

Nor did the jurors fail to recall how news of birth and baptism of the heir were an occasion for rejoicing, and we have memories of how both those in the baby's family and those among their friends might have expressed pleasure upon hearing the good news. When a servant told Lord Bonville of his son's birth, "rejoicing he raised his hands in thanks to God and immediately ... rode home." One juror had been treated to a meal of red wine and roast goose—probably well beyond the resources of his own table—when he brought the good news and the father "saying that he thanked God for sending him an heir." Friends and well-wishers could be very public about the rejoicing after a safe birth. Upon hearing that all had gone well, Henry Percy, knight, welcomed the new babe, "at which Henry was exceedingly joyful." A more detailed one of these "good news" memories came from a Proof from Newcastle upon Tyne: the juror said he had seen the baby's grandfather meet a woman who was carrying the baby to church and the grandfather said to the woman, "'May I ask you to show me the infant?' which she did and he kissed him and said 'God bless you my son, and may He give you health and strength on earth' (*dixit ei filii mi deum te benedicat et det tibi et bonam vigenciam in terra*)." In this same Proof another juror added that the priest had said "*Deo gracias* because now William Mitford has an heir of his name."[3] It might be the cleric who wished to emphasize the importance of the event, as well as to assert his privileged status touching sacramental matters, and when a juror said he had brought news of Joan's birth to a monk of Torre Abbey, the latter "joyfully said 'come to the church and give thanks to Almighty God!' ... He also asked John (the juror) not to leave the church until he saw the infant baptized."[4] In a world of difficult deliveries and high mortality a safe birth and a healthy child were indeed a matter of gratification. Three elderly jurors recalled how they had blessed the newborn: "They went to the church for the baptism, saying they hoped that Nicholas would prove as good a fighting man as his godfather."[5] One of the most effusive statements of congratulation and a blessing came from the baby's grandfather—as told by a juror, 46 years and more—remember how when the grandfather met a woman carrying the baby he said "'May I ask you to show me the infant?' which she did, and he kissed him and said 'God bless you, my son, and may He give you health and strength on earth' (*dixit ei filii mi deus te benedicat et det tibi et bonam vigenciam in terra*)."[6]

Organizing and analyzing the memories that centered on birth and baptism takes us back to the realm of big numbers—414 Proofs and thousands of jurors and jurors' memories. In numerical terms most Proofs—and perhaps about half of all the memories—touch on the acts and scenes that, from start to finish, constitute what we refer to as the ritual and/or the drama of the baptism. Few Proofs are without any memories of this sort, wherever else our 12 men may take us in their brief moment on stage. In Chap. 2 we addressed the key question that the escheator put to the 12 jurors: "how do you remember something that happened 21 (or 14, or 16) years ago?" As we now work our way through the separate scenes of the drama of birth and baptism, we can look at the various ways in which each juror grounded his testimony.

How did he frame his mnemonic to give it the requisite air of authoritative knowledge and recollection? There are a number of answers to this. We have those memories that rest on the coincidence of close timing between the heir's baptism and something in his own life: "I remember the date of the baptism because my sister died then" or "that was when I went on pilgrimage to Canterbury" or "while going home from church I saw a tree fall over." Such statements needed no further elaboration; they were just accepted as belonging to the juror's world of lived experience and if that was what he chose to offer, he had done his duty. Many memories rest on the juror's active participation in the ceremony of interest here: "I held the baby by the font" or "I was sent to fetch the priest." His personal experiences were his but now they were being shared with his fellow jurors and toward a common purpose, even if his role had hardly been a key one (though it sometimes was). Then there were memories based on what he had seen, even if he had not been an active participant: "I saw the baby lifted from the font" being fairly common, given the central position of the parish church and the likelihood that the baby's baptism drew a large congregation as an all-village event. Then there were memories of things heard, that is, of being told: "We were at dinner and a messenger told us of the baby's baptism" or "I was told by people returning from the baptism that the ceremony had been held." And since all the jurors' memories were accepted and all the Proofs "voted" for the heir as now being of age, the distinctions we have drawn here were of little relevance, or even noted, at the time. While we might think that the best memories were those of jurors who had been active participants, including those who had been godparents, this is a distinction that does not really distinguish. Clearly, one memory was as good as another, with no preference accorded the unusual or the idiosyncratic over the most run-of-the-mill recollections.

The drama of "birth and baptism" opens with several scenes that—linked together as they are—comprise the first act. Act I, scene i, opens with activities that centered around the need to "call the midwife," and Act I, scene ii draws on memories touching the mother in labor and afterward (though her churching will be covered as one of the closing scenes). Scholarly interest in midwives and midwifery—how these women fended off the intrusion of male doctors and their fight to retain their medical and social status—falls well outside any memories offered in the Proofs. The world of obstetrics and gynecology was very much a women's world—not for men's memories—though we do get glimpses of rivalry between competing practitioners and we encounter sensible requests for the most experienced and most trustworthy.[7] The medieval scene of birthing is a familiar one, depicted in the illustrations for such as the birth of the Virgin, with St. Anne decorously lying in childbed while a well-swaddled infant resides comfortably in the arms of one of the well-dressed midwives or maids who stand by the bedside. Sometimes there might be men around, though if so they are safely stationed well in the background. A scene, no doubt, based on the realities of the day, and not many of our jurors add much to this basic picture. Nor, we note, is there any sign of a wet nurse in the depictions of the sacred birth, in contrast to the reverent depictions of Mary herself nursing the baby Jesus. We know the ease with which the Virgin gave birth and we trust that her mother had a comparably easy time.

As the end of pregnancy neared it was time to summon the various troops who would carry us into the forthcoming scenes of the drama, with the midwife being first in the queue. Though presumably preparations had already been made—pregnancy rarely being much of a secret—it must have been an urgent call for her services that sparked one juror's memory, as he had been "in bed with his wife Agnes on the day of the birth when Thomas Taberwell came at dawn to ask her to be midwife to Elizabeth the mother." Though her role as midwife is not specified, this may have been what was meant in the memories of a woman, as recounted by her husband; she had been sent to "see how Maurice was kept and nursed" or of when "Margaret his wife was asked at the time of Thomas's birth to help Thomas's mother." From one of the urban Proofs we learn of "Albreda, wife of Richard Sutton, citizen and stockfishmonger of London, [who] was sought to wash and attend John." Several men told of learning of the baby's birth by having met the midwife on her way home after she had done her duty: he met "the common midwife in those parts" and she carried the baby, "wrapped in a fine cloth," presumably on their way to church for the baptism. For a midwife who came prepared for something other than the usual problems of the birth chamber, we can offer Isabel Harper, "midwife, and she brought a comb for William as soon as she saw him born because he had a hairy head." And though the messenger summoning the midwife was usually welcomed and often rewarded, as were various messengers who play a part in other scenes of the drama, this seemingly safe and peripheral (and male) role might carry some risk, as it did for the juror who had been sent to fetch the midwife "to help Hugh's mother during the birth" but who, because of a slippery path, "fell and broke his knee and his ankle." The baby's birthday would have been well remembered by our would-be messenger, as he "was often burdened by this misfortune afterwards."[8] Nor was he without companions in this lugubrious tale: sent for the midwife, another juror "went in the morning before it was light. Crossing a stream by a little bridge, he fell in the stream and was severely chilled [*infrigidatus*]."[9] But as it was women's business, it seems fitting that *she* at least escaped more serious harm: 'the mid-wife who was carrying Joan. A great oak standing before the door ... fell, [and] a branch hit the mid-wife and she only just escaped with her life."[10]

Some jurors offered a more personal memory of the baby's birth, though the wording may not have been taken as literally as it seems to read. Was he really as much part of the action as he implied: "he knows this [the heir's age] because he was at Tremedont [Cornwall] when Amice mother of John was in labour and he heard her crying. Before he withdrew, she gave birth." A more decorous juror remembered that he had "heard her cry but then he withdrew."[11] At least it was secondhand knowledge in the memory of the juror who had "heard Margery ... labour and cry out especially for her child's delivery, and early in the morning of 13 August. He knew through Joan his wife, that Margery had that night been delivered of an infant." Women's world—women's business: "Margaret his wife was present at Joan's birth and told him that Joan was born in that vill..." though in his statement he says that "he saw him [the heir] at the breast (*lactantem matricem suam*) immediately after birth." Had he crossed into feminine space, as perhaps had been the case with a juror who also "knows because he saw him born."[12]

These memories bespeak a safe delivery and the overall impression is that most of the upper-class mothers giving birth came through the ordeal, though not always. One man remembered that "Alice's mother died the day after Alice was born."[13] Other women must have had some near misses; the juror recalled meeting "his niece who told him that Isabel mother of William was in danger of dying," though we have no follow-up on her fate, nor do we know what happened with another new mother who was in danger, as we learn from a juror who had gone "to the house of John Clervaux the grandfather to see the child's mother, who was very ill."[14] A gift of 40d. from the juror's wife to "Joan, mother of John, who was weak from his birth," almost sounds like an effort to placate evil spirits.[15] Was another juror referring to the mother, shortly after she had given birth, or was he talking of the celebration at the time of her churching: he "heard that Lady Katherine had given birth to a son. To comfort her in her convalescence he offered her a gift of a partridge." But another man, testifying in that same Proof, had "heard that Lady Katherine had recovered from her pregnancy," which sounds like we are closer to the birth moment in these memories than we are to the festivities of a month or so later.[16] Mostly though, it was a good time, and we can look to the juror who talked again about disseminating the news. It was "announced that William had a beautiful first-born son by his wife Elizabeth, daughter of John Moigne, knight and all present rejoined."[17]

After a safe birth, at least for the baby, baptism was in order—the next scene of the drama. Being sent to bring in the leading cast members was a task often given to the jurors—a sign of their middling status and, seemingly, of their trustworthiness—and we have memories referring to their vital role in getting the troops in line. In one memory it was the priest, clearly harassed by the need to handle more than one obligations: two jurors told of when "they were along towards the church ... [and they] met the parish clerk running for the vicar to visit and confess John de Deppyng, then in extremis, who died the same day about the hour of vespers."[18] Not as needed for sacramental purposes but presumably of some domestic value, there was the father: the juror "on that day was sent to London [from Buckingham] by Margaret, Lady Moleyns, to discover where John the father could be found."[19]

One set of men and women were needed for this most basic of Christian rituals and sacraments—the godparents—while another set of women—the nurses or wet nurses—were needed for the care of the infant. If "fetch the midwife" was a theme we have just touched on, then "fetch the godparents" along with "fetch the wet nurse" now became the orders of the day, coming perhaps on the heels of memories of "fetch the father" and "fetch the priest." And whatever we might offer about a child's health and nutrition, in spiritual and social terms it was the godparents who took precedence over the nurse who would be enlisted to feed, swaddle, and rock the infant. Nothing could happen until the pieces were all in place, as four jurors who had been servants in the father's house attested: "the first three were sent to get the godfather and godmothers, and John Karsewyll [one of the four] was sent to get the parish chaplain of the church, to fulfill their roles in the baptism."[20] The godparents are often named by that first juror, he who seemed to be a *de facto* foreman, as part of his opening statement and perhaps as a sign that he really remembered what he was about to attest. The names of the two men and one woman, for a male heir, or the reverse in numbers were she a girl, gave credibility to this first juror's memory, though we have no way of explaining the memory of Roger Hillom, he having been "present in the church and saw him [the baby] having 4 godfathers and 2 godmothers whence there was a multiplicity of promises."[21] As we have noted above, memories of the baptism provided jurors with an opportunity to indulge in some name dropping, as in the Proof where the key roles of the earl Arundel as one godfather and William de Monte Acuto, earl of Salisbury, were mentioned more than once. When the heir was Richard Beauchamp, future earl of Warwick, the jurors told of seeing some of the attending celebrities: Henry Wakefield, bishop of Worcester (who had done the baptizing); the prior or abbots of Worcester, Evesham, and Pershore; John Beauchamp of Holt; and the earl himself. John Beauchamp came "carrying 2 cloths of gold with the arms (*de exeunte*) of King Richard."[22]

Choosing the baby's godparents was an important choice that fell to the parents and we have memories that tell of the jurors themselves being asked to stand in for this role, as well as their more frequent memories of others who had been so chosen.[23] Given the sex of the heirs, we have more godfathers than godmothers, though the women, and their vital role, are also remembered. One juror recalled when he had "met Joan Meny who told him that she was one of the said Isabel's god-mothers and had just come from Hatton Church where she had been baptized that day." The baby's name was usually worked out in advance, though here too it occasionally was a matter of indecision or even of dispute, seemingly up to the last moment. One juror recalled that he had been a godfather to Thomas and "was told to name him Thomas after his great-grandfather," prior instructions of this sort being very common and a wise precaution. One man recalled that his brother "was diligently asked … at the time of Elizabeth's birth to name Elizabeth at the font." We know that godparents were often chosen because they bore the name the parents wished to bestow on the newborn. We see this is in a Proof where a cleric was the baby's uncle and he "was godfather and called him [the baby] Robert after Robert de Roos, his ancestor."[24] This explains why there had been some surprise because "Henry [Beaumont] did not bear the same name as his god-father, Thomas la Warre," the godfather here perhaps choosing to follow in the footsteps of the father of John the Baptist. Though the baptism was a solemn ritual and naming the child something that usually indicated some planning in advance, one memory seems to reveal a last-minute aspect to the ceremony, making us wonder if on some occasions one godfather was considered to be much like the next. A juror said that he had gone "to the house of Hugh Kynder to buy an ox. Now Hugh was starting for the parish church ... to be the heir's god-father, and because he stayed too long a certain Robert Hyde became god-father."[25] Clearly, the ceremony was not to be postponed because of Hugh's absence nor was the original choice for the godfather so critical that his absence could put a stop to the proceedings. Nor, it seems, did the last-minute substitution of a "Robert" for a "Hugh" cause a problem.

Among the memories that focus on the identity and role of the godparents we have some references to impediments, quarrels, and mishaps, all marring what was meant to be a day of joy and celebration. Some memories open a window on the competition people might feel regarding being asked to stand in this honorable and responsible position regarding the newborn. One man said that he had been asked to be a godfather, but "although he wished to be a god-father he refused because such a spiritual relationship could, in future, be an impediment to marriage," thereby showing an acquaintance with canon law regarding that sprawling web of forbidden kinships created by baptismal sponsorship. Another juror related a personal experience that may have left a bad taste, for "on the same day [of the heir's baptism] he asked Robert, abbot of Myddelton, to take his son from the baptismal font but the abbot could not do so because on that day he was to be godfather to the said heir." Did the abbot feel prohibited from performing two baptisms on the same day or was this an excuse to avoid a task he was not inclined to carry out?[26] The abbot of Missenden was an exalted choice for a godfather, though he "had an illness called 'le collyk' and could hardly act."[27] A juror in Devon remembered that the father of the babe had asked him to stand as her godfather, "but he could not ride because of various infirmities."[28]

Nor did being in the church necessarily guarantee harmony among the participants. One juror "heard Anne's godmothers arguing about Anne's name ... and they agreed to name her Anne because she was born on the

feast of that saint."[29] Nor were such differences confined to the godmothers. The juror "knows [the age of the heir] because Thomas abbot of
Croxton and Roger Belers, knight ... were the heir's god-fathers, and
there was a dispute between them as to which of them had named him
first, whereupon by unanimous consent they named him William, as most
of his ancestors were named" and it is no wonder that this odd affair stuck
in the memory.[30] To give these memories a more irenic flavor, we have the
juror who saw Lionel's god-mother, Alice Deroy, give him a silver bowl
when he was baptized; gifts from godparent were probably expected.[31]
And just as we had a Proof in which the jurors said they could tell more
about the heir's age, were it necessary to do so, now we have a juror who
offers another of these tantalizing and elusive memories. When he had
been asked by the father to stand in as the baby's godfather, "he excused
himself for a secret reason which he told him [the father]."[32] Whatever the
secret, it died with the juror.[33]

The seriousness of the honor involved in being part of the naming process comes through in one of the longest of all the depositions, one also
shedding light on local interest in kinship networks and on the important
households of the area. No fewer than three men, in a common memory,
attest that they know the heir's age because

> they were at Honiton [Devon] for a loveday to settle a dispute ... and
> there came Lady Katharine, formerly the wife of John, Cobham, knight,
> and then the wife of John Wyke of Nynehead, aunt of William, proposing
> to ride to Shute and expecting to be godmother of William [the baby].
> There she met Edward Dygher, a servant of William Bonevile, knight,
> whom half seriously she reproached for being merry and talkative. He
> asked where she was going. To which she replied quickly that she was
> going to Shute to make her nephew a Christian. Grinning he answered in
> his mother tongue 'Kate, Kate, ther to by myn pate comyst ow to late'
> because the baptism is performed. Mounting her horse again she rode
> home very angry, not seeing the child's mother again for 6 months. And
> this all the jurors know.[34]

Lady Katherine, we would say, "had been dissed" and she was not shy
about letting others know. There had been none of those last-minute
"fetch the godmother" in this case, though such late efforts were hardly
unknown.

On to the next scene of the drama, as the pieces fall into place and at
least most of the cast were there to await their turn. Though she stood in

a lesser position in terms of honor and drama, the wet nurse was, in terms of life and survival, a good deal more vital to the process of raising the baby than were the godparents. Because her duties might involve a relatively long-term commitment we sometimes have a juror who talks of her remuneration (from the baby's parents, not from the juror). This worldly matter was something never alluded to in the numerous midwife memories, though presumably she too had been rewarded in the coin of the realm or through a payment in kind. But before the wet nurse was paid, she had to be found (and hired): "Maurice was placed to nurse with the wife of John Jann, carpenter," which also speaks of the social gap between the infant and the nurse. Was the payment fair when "Ralph Cromwell, grandfather of Anne, told him [the juror] to give the midwife 20s?" One woman may have done better, though it seemingly was a case of more money to match a longer commitment: "Margaret his wife became the nurse of Miles on the day of his birth. She was hired for a whole year, and Richard gave her 40s. stipend." Moreover, even when the date of birth was correctly called, the hiring of the wet nurse might be a last-minute affair. The memory of a juror "that he had been sent for Margaret Reynewall to be John's wet nurse immediately after John was baptised" argues for a brief interval between birth and baptism.[35] If one wanted a wet nurse with good credentials, one presumably had to be willing to pay: William Lumbard remembered "because Isabel wife of John Roudon sent for him ... [and] she said 'Your wife is the best nurse in these parts, so I ask that she care for the son of Margaret my daughter. I will reward her for this work and service' ... William entered the church to see the son. He saw the parson baptizing him and naming him John ... He immediately returned to Isabel, saying that the son was exceedingly handsome and that he wanted to talk to his wife about satisfying Isabel's request. Isabel gave him a gold coin." We assume John's wife accepted the offer.[36] One woman boasted to a juror that she "had a tenement in Harringworth by gift of William the father," which seems far beyond the ordinary going return for a nurse's services.[37] Moreover, while this was very much a woman's world, at least one memory was from a juror who had, with the midwife and other women, consulted among themselves to find "a good wet nurse."[38]

The birth might come before all the planning had been completed: "his wife was sought at night at the time of Lionel's birth to nurse and wet nurse him (*ad lactandum et nutriendum*)," with the double duty being understood.[39] Sometimes it could be a case of one family's misfortune working to the advantage of another, as it was for a juror who spoke of when "his wife Margaret, after the death of their daughter Isabel, was Robert de la Doune's nurse; and Isabel died on the feast of the nativity of the Virgin following," so the date stuck in the juror's memory.[40] Because the use of the wet nurse was so widespread, and because her role was considered important for the health and future deportment of the infant, other conditions and circumstances affecting the wet nurse are occasionally spoken of. Men might be enlisted in the search for "the best." One juror recalled when he had "had a discussion with the midwife and other women through which they found a good wet nurse," and in a comparable memory it was that he had "found her a nurse who stayed with her until she was weaned."[41] It seems clear that having a man—the juror himself, usually, in these memories—be involved in the discussion of whom to hire was perfectly acceptable. And on the idea that the employer could impose conditions on the employee, we have the juror who remembered that "his wife Isabel was John's nurse for three years afterward and that on the day of John's baptism he left Dartington for Guernsey because John de Holand, the father of John brother of Richard, forbade him to have marital relations with Isabel during that time."[42] On a more domestic note, a young juror, in a Proof for a 14-year-old heiress, told of when "Isabel, his wife was Alice's nurse on that day and for a long time afterwards, and he saw her in her cradle."[43]

* * *

In keeping with the idea that the baptism of a (high born) baby was a highly visible drama of many acts and with several scenes within each act, it seems but fitting, before we go onto the main stage, to look at the assembling of the properties—the props—without which no drama, let alone a historical costume drama, could proceed. Here most of the relevant memories are simple references to how the juror—and here it was usually a memory of a juror's own role—had been instructed to help with the various implements and artifacts, the paraphernalia, needed for the ceremony. What this survey of the props does, beyond giving a quick inventory of what was called for in the church for the ceremony, is to remind us of how many people, of varying stations and skills, became involved in this *rite de passage* for an infant who might well become the ruling figure of the region. The whole ceremony surrounding baptism was not just drama or theater, but was "public theater" with both a team of actors and an audience of villagers, many of whom will step forward years later to tell of the role they played (or to claim a role they may have played). Many jurors fell back on a memory of having been personally involved: they had carried "a basin and ewer full of water to church to wash the hands of the godfathers and godmother," or had been instructed to bring "flame and water," or "salt in a silver salt-cellar, and a towel to go with it," or "a wax candle to burn before the image of the Virgin Mary."[44] There was more of this: "a consecrated candle (*cereuni benedictum*)," or "bread and two silver pots full of sweet wine called 'osey'" or "two silver pots of clary and malmsey and four goblets ... to drink that day," or we have the juror who had "carried miller cake for the godfathers and god-mothers with sweet wine to strengthen them," or it might be "a kynderkyn of ale" or "bread and two silver pots of sweet wine."[45] With all the water used in the ceremony, the value of a "cloth for drying of hands after the baptism" seemed a sensible item to have ready. One memory touched on the practical side of all this preparation, coming from the juror, a "skinner," who had sold the grandfather "for 100s. a pure grey fur in which John was wrapped when carried to church."[46] And looking back to that monk who had steered the villagers to church to rejoice in the baby's safe birth, he also sent John, our juror, "to find fire, water, salt, and other necessities for the baptism."[47] It was seemly for the proud father to spend money on the great occasion, and a Newcastle juror looked back on "that day [when he] sold to William Mitford an ell of light cloth (*una ulna panni leuij*) called 'Clothe of lake' for a 'Crissomclosth' to be made for John Mitford."[48]

In keeping with all this preparation it was only fitting that the parish church itself be decorated for the ceremony, though we might think that the 24 men with 24 candles of one juror's recollection to be a bit excessive.[49] A parish church might well have become a bit cluttered, as for the two jurors who recalled that "a candlestick fell on their heads when they were in the church at the time of the baptism," though they seem to have escaped serious injury.[50] We have reports of the church being "adorned with cloth of silk and gold and the font hung with a cloth of gold decorated in red." One man had been sent to make sure the church was ready for the ceremony and he remembered that he had gone "to the church and found it decorated with four gold cloths around the altar and the font finely decorated with cloths of white silk ... all was prepared."[51] But there were always pitfalls and we have a grouchy recollection from the juror who had "made a wax candle weighing 2lb on that day to burn and hold in the church at Thomas's baptism, for which he has not yet been paid."[52] Was he better off than the man who "brought the chrism for the high altar … to the font, and as he returned to the altar he tripped over a bench in the church for which he was badly laughed at afterwards?"[53]

The baptism itself was the sacred (as well as social) moment at the font. Though the priest usually seems to have been on the spot and ready to do his duty—it being a special occasion for him as well as for baby and family—there seem to have been times when "fetch the priest" was still the memory being offered. This was the memory of a juror who recalled that he "went to find John Preston, the chaplain, and [he] made him come to the church, and was himself present," or that of the man who, "on that day met Margaret's father going to Camberwell on a bay horse to find the vicar to baptize her."[54] Far from Camberwell, a Proof from Cumberland and touching the high-and-mighty: two jurors, "servants of William Dacre, knight, [who] were sent that day to the vicar of Brampton to warn him for the baptism and they were present in the church."[55]

Some memories of the baptism come from the jurors who themselves had played—or claimed to have played—an active role in some phase of the ceremony. But most of the hundreds of relevant memories were of things seen or words heard: the babe at the font, the words of the priest, a request from the father to the priest for the date to be written down, the role of the godparents, the wrapping of the baby, the baby being carried to or from church, and so on. Some men (and women; coming through as secondhand information) had come to church to witness the ceremony. Others happened to be in church—witnesses by coincidence or inadvertence—but they were still firm in offering a memory of the event. Whether he came expressly for the baptism or not, one juror was there for what he must have considered as a special event: he had been "in the church while all the chaplains and clerky sang a solemn *Te Deum*," perhaps as part of a thanksgiving for safe birth.[56] Those who came to church for some other purpose remind us that a baptism might well coincide with other events and services, given the many uses of the parish church. Men might come there to arrange their own family ceremony or for a sacramental occasion like a marriage, or to meet with colleagues to set off on a pilgrimage, or for participating in a love-day, or for secular business in what served as the village hall as well as the house of worship.

Into the church: sacrament and ritual, social ceremony and a community event, all wrapped up in one. Many jurors' memories of the baptism focus on that act of writing—that is, of the baby's birthdate being set to writing in some service book or other. We said above that writing-based memories are not only common but that they seemed to carry and convey a special aura of credibility, a recognition that to write something down was to give it a privileged anchorage against the erosion of time and memory. In a few cases, but only in a few, the juror indicated that he himself had done the writing. One man recalled his role, his agency, in the writing-and-dating process: he had been "asked by god-parents to record the day of Giles's birth in the same missal and received 12d. for doing so." But most writing-inspired memories were of the "things seen" or "things heard" category; the juror heard a request to the priest, coming from the father or a godparent, or perhaps the juror indicated that he had seen the priest in the act of writing. Two jurors, in a joint memory, had seen the priest "write the date in a missal in their presence and that of several others." While the act of priestly writing was described in much the same way in all these memories, the service book or sacred book in which the information had been recorded varied from account to account. One juror recounted a memory of when "the father then asked the then rector to write the day and year of the birth in a martyrology, and so it is now recorded and they know the date." It might be "the day and place of birth [written] in a great breviary of the church." One juror had not seen the act of writing while in church but he had seen "the abbot show a book in which this date of the birth was entered"—the juror not being asked to write but rather to "witness to the age of Richard, and that he might thereby have and enjoy his father's lands and tenements."[57] In a reference to what we would label the public gaze, one memory is of four men who came to church together ("to make offering before a picture of the Virgin Mary") and "when the parson was baptizing, and [they] saw him write the date in a missal in their presence and that of several others, and so they know the date."[58] In that same Proof another juror said he had been asked by the baby's uncle and godfather to write "the time of the birth in books of John Boson, Geoffrey Deen, Thomas Mayhewe and others," a memory that shines light on both lay literacy and book ownership. Nor were all these memories happy ones, and one man remembered because "his son Robert died at about 6 a.m. He went to the church to summon the parson to come and perform Robert's obsequie and he saw him baptize John, and write his name in a book."[59] For a memory that reveals some of that pride surrounding literacy, one man recalled that "the grandfather invited him to admire the record of John's age in the missal because his son Alexander

acted as William's clerk [William being the grandfather] and wrote his letters and other private business."[60]

Things seen, things heard, things remembered. One juror recalled the
he had "heard the rector order the clerk of the church to enroll William's
name and time of his birth in the book of benefactors [*martilagium*] of
the church as a perpetual memorial of the birth." The presiding clerics
might be asked, usually by the father, to record the event: "the father
asked the parson to write in a missal in English, 'And ... Nycol the sone of
John ate Hall and Crystyne his wife was y bore'." The vernacular was
beginning to declare itself: "the date was written in English in a book and
read out whilst they (two jurors) were there," seemingly telling the
assembled congregation that the vital information was now safely enshrined
in written form.[61] One memory went back to the birth date being entered
into "a church Bible," and another man summed up the value of the written record with a terse "the writing is still there."[62] Other writings are
mentioned—other books: the Bible, held in the hands of the parish clerk
at her baptism, the martyrology, where "it is now recorded and they know
the date": "a great breviary of the church."[63] The emphasis on the written
record may indicate that the parents of the heirs were more at ease with
literacy than the jurors, though the latter also seem at ease when the memory they offered ran in that direction.

Baptism would have been a familiar business, even in the most isolated
of parish churches. Memories of the baby, lifted from the font and wrapped
in protective clothing by godparents or other well-wishers, were a stock in
trade among the Proofs and we have hundreds of memories that attest to
the simple fact, the *fait accompli*, recalled by those who had observed the
act of baptism.[64] Once in a while we have a reference to a glitch or an
unplanned moment. A bit more detail, as when the juror recalled that he
saw the vicar "wrap him in a linen clothe called 'crism' marked at the head
with a cross of red and gold silk" and that it had been on the feast of St.
Agatha was but an additional detail.[65] Another man probably reveled in
what may have been the high moment of his village status in another of
those oft-told tales. He had been in church and "observing that the holy
water clerk was absent ... [off] to visit his sick mother, he [the juror] performed all the necessary duties of the holy water clerk and saw the baptism."[66] One juror offered that the baptism in question was the first in the
new font, clearly an opportune moment at which to introduce a high-born
infant to the flock of Christ's sheep. Minor accidents were not unheard of:
"as the parson who had baptized her was lowering the font cover it fell to

the ground and was badly damaged. Afterwards they drank wine…" so presumably there had been no serious casualties. The baby might play an unexpected role, as one juror remembered, he having been "present in the church at the baptism … and saw him [the infant] lift his right hand and take the said Philippa [the godmother] by her veil."[67] The infant was not always at her or his most sociable, as we learn from the juror who "saw Humphrey urinating in the font" or from the man who "was in the church for mass on the same day and heard John's most frequent crying caused by the cold water."[68] It seems to have worked out without serious consequences when "John fell from the chaplain's hands into the font and John Wedryngton, knight, John's god-father, then said to the chaplain, 'Prest, prest, fond be thi hened'."[69] But memory served to preserve these moments, though there seems to be a touch of making do with whatever was at hand when the "record of John's birth [was recorded] in the table of contents of his psalter."[70] No harm, as well, when "the holy water clerk broke the lamp before the high altar and the oil fell on his head."[71]

Many memories of the baptism were from afar, that is they were offered by men who happened to have seen—and who now remembered—the procession. There are hundreds of these, much in the same vein, though usually with fewer details, as the common memory of six men. They had been "practicing archery in a field by the churchyard and saw Christine [the mid-wife] carrying the baby from the church in Itchen to cross the river Itchen in a boat called 'le Passeger' to the manor of Woolston."[72] It would seem that since the baptism the key link in the chain, even an impersonal or distant involvement in this was a good memory. Also, being part of a crowd is always a credible way to station oneself regarding time and place.

Beyond those who "saw" from a distance are the memories of jurors who just happened to be in church for some other reason than for the baptism but who nevertheless were witnesses. Such memories give us an idea of the many *other* reasons there were for being in the building. Some of these other activities clearly fit into the church's role in the community: to arrange or attend a wedding or a funeral or to do homage to an image. Some men, as we have indicated, used the church as a meeting place for business, though they were happy to stand up years later and contribute a memory that helps pin down the time of the baptism. There was parish business, recalled by a man who had been there "to account for the church's goods which they [he and two colleagues] had in their custody as church wardens," while another offered a different kind of spiritually oriented memory in recalling that "on the same day the parishioners there bought an image of the Blessed Mary which is still in the church."[73] One pair of churchwardens said they had rendered their account of the goods "bequeathed to St Mary ... at divers times, as is enrolled in the missal there," to give a different slant on the practical role of the written word as a guide to memory.[74] Though we will turn to pilgrimage memories below, the church could serve as a convenient rendezvous point, as it did for the three men who had been about to set out for Santiago and "they were in the church ... to take leave of their neighbours when they saw the said heir baptized."[75]

Other ceremonies and other sacraments offered useful memories. A marriage could be arranged with more certainty than birth and baptism, and this ceremony had brought several jurors to church: one man "was at the espousal of James Seybon, servant of John Bedenham, esquire" when the baptism took place, while another was himself married "on the day that she was baptized and [he] waited at the church door during her baptism."[76] It could be the most pedestrian of coincidences, as for the juror who "was at the church to hear mass before going to buy fish at Bootle, and was present at the baptism." Or it could have been a painful memory of the kind of loss we will expand on below: "William Elyot ... says that on that day, for lack of care by her nurse, his daughter named Walkelina suddenly died of thirst in her cradle. For this reason he came to the church ... to ask the parson to say divine services for his daughter's soul and saw the parson writing while Philip was baptized... The memory of this misfortune has never left him."[77]

Where better than in the parish church for the resolution of a quarrel and for the love-day that put it all to rights? It must have been quite serious for the parties involved, since we get the memory as a common one from five men who "were in the crypt under the church when an agreement was made between Richard Gargrave, 'bowyer', and Thomas Clyve, 'goldsmyth', following a long dispute between them. A day for reconciliation had been appointed and an arbiter for each chosen ... after agreement was reached ... they came before the mayor and John Castell in the church after John's baptism and had the arbitration enrolled."[78] A comparable memory, if less detailed but still as told in unison by four jurors, "all [were] in church, saw the baptism and settled various disputes"; a tribute to the church as a house of many uses.[79] Quarrels between men of the cloth were reported, though it was their resolution that jurors remembered: disputes of "tithes of wools" and "tithes of lambs," the last one between a prior and a vicar.[80] One of the more unusual memories, and without reference to a dispute, takes us to the world of popular piety and clerical erudition—an aspect of life rarely mentioned in a proof—coming here from ten men in a joint memory. They had been "congregated in the church, standing there among many others to hear a sermon by master Robert Hardyng, doctor of theology, and they saw Thomas Woller, chaplain, godfather, write the day and year of his birth in the missal books of the church ... which they subsequently inspected."[81]

The drama begins to wind down, the last few acts perhaps being rather anticlimactic after the baptism itself. Some of the after-the-ritual memories were of those from men sent out to carry the news of birth and baptism. Sometimes these were the jurors, sometimes we have secondhand tales recounting a warm welcome and a reward. The rewards, at least as recalled years later, were certainly generous, with perhaps a touch of exaggeration, and it was at secondhand that a juror knew that "Peter Holt received £10 for taking the news to the earl," while another man—also in a secondhand memory—had been "shown 100s. in gold by William Chamberlayne who had been given it by John the father for being first to bring him the news."[82] One new father had generously shared a recent windfall, as he had "received £23 4s. 4d. from his reeve for wool sold, and out of reverence for God's gratitude for the birth of the boy gave him, John [the juror and the messenger] £3 4s. 4d."[83] In one well-phrased memory, the paternal grandmother "gave him 2 gold nobles, such things he had never had before."[84] Or it might be new clothing: "he had a red gown, price 26s. 8d. for his labour," or he "brought him [the father] news of the birth for which he was given a tunic."[85] Setting another place at the table for someone who normally would not have been invited was also a memorable way of having been rewarded, as with the juror who recalled that "they asked him to eat roast goose at the table with them and to share the red wine ... saying he [the father] thanked God for sending him an heir."[86] But moving above oneself carried its dangers, as accepted by the juror who was "staying with the heir's father and for joy at the heir's birth became so drunk he fell down and broke his leg."[87]

We near the final curtain: memories of the churching of the mother and then a grab-bag of memories about more gifts to the babe and/or to the mother. Churching was a formal ceremony, another significant *rite de passage* in a mother's journey through Christian life. In a strict sense it was at least in good part a matter of the women's world, though men did share in the good tidings and gave gifts to the mother—as godparents and others had given to the babe—as a signal of her welcome return to full social, sexual, and sacramental life. Though the churching was expected to take place around 40 days after birth, some detailed memories tell of a shorter interval. In a number of Proofs from Essex in the 1420s we have memories that assert that the juror, accompanying his wife, had been around for both the birth and the churching. The intervals between the birth as dated in the Proof and the ceremony might be 24 days, or 39, or 25, and then 24 again.[88] Perhaps both the new mothers and their social and domestic circle were eager for her return to normality.

Some memories about the churching tell of the festivities that accompanied the ceremony. One such did focus on the sacramental side of the business: "on Sunday, a month after the said 20 November they saw Joyce, the heir's mother, purified of her said boy."[89] Mostly, though, the memories relate to the trappings of the ceremony: jurors had sold meats to the father for a banquet, or it could have been the clothes "in which she was churched," or the men who recalled that they had sold red gascon wine or perhaps it had been a red cow, or those sent to deliver a gown and a dress to the new mother.[90] It could be a memorable occasion: "they ate in the hall ... on the occasion of the getting up (*resureccione*) of the said Fulk's mother." And here too, one man who had hoped to get involved in the festivities came to grief: "long before she was churched he went for doves to send her ... [he] fell from the ladder, near the top, broke his right arm and was badly crushed."[91] One of his fellow jurors may have had mixed feelings, for on the day of the churching of the heir's mother his own mother-in-law died and "he succeeded to all her lands ... in right of Alice" [his wife]. The best we can ask is that he would have been ambivalent when he looked back to the day.

Gifts to the baby and/or to the new mother are hardly a surprise. What is of interest, as we categorize these memories, is that the giving of the gift was still, in many instances, the memorable feature to recall. Some of our jurors' one-liners talk of a gift to the baby, others to the mother, and gifts coming from aristocratic relatives and godparents could be of considerable value, apart from any of the sentimental message they might carry. One fairly standard memory ran thus: the juror had seen "Alice Circase, the god-mother, give Thomas [the baby] a silver bowl and his nurse 6s.," or he had seen "Kenelm, parson ... [and] god-father, give Ralph a silver goblet with a cover soon after he was baptized and his nurse 6s. 8d."[92] An interesting variation is that these gifts might take the form of meat as a gift: game, in most cases, but not always. In the proof of the heir to an earldom, the juror said that he had, "on that day brought 12 partridges to Thomas de Holland," and others in that same jury told of offering two swans, to the mother, and a wild boar to the father.[93] There were other memories of this sort, some with a bit more detail, with a successful hunt worth a mention. One man, out in the fields, "saw a sitting hare, shot it in the head with an arrow, and sent it to Beatrice [the mother] on the day of the birth."[94] This was on a level with the gift from a juror who "was in Knaresborough forest the day after the birth and killed a great stag. He sent it to Thomas and Eleanor" [the parents].[95] We can judge the generosity of the man who "fished in the river Eden and caught 40 salmon, of which he gave four to Elizabeth's mother."[96] In another touch of "merrie England," one juror recalled that he had "caught two partridges with his hawk and sent them to the mother."[97] Gifts like these would have had an immediate practical use, given the obligation on the part of the parents to play host to guests who had come specifically for the event, alongside all those folks of the village who were more than happy to mark the occasion by its free food and drink. And at the high end, as godfather the Duke of Gloucester gave had "a golden reliquary with precious stones and a picture of the Trinity," as befit his rank, wealth, and role in the baptism.[98] That gifts were frequently offered, and frequently remembered, even if they did not match the duke's generosity, is a comforting domestic note on which to draw a sheet over these baptism-related memories, they all coming to rest on the social and spiritual routines and rituals that marked the entry of a new member of Christ's church and of the king's realm.

Notes

1. 2 24/270.
2. 3 24/169. Though the different wording probably reflects no difference in meaning, "made a Christian" seems to give more agency to those who performed the ceremony (22/223). Good wording: "Joan was baptised and a Christian" (24/208).
3. 4 22/358.
4. 22/130: 19/997: 22/358: 25/298.
5. 20/272. This is a rather tangled Proof because the baby's paternal grandmother died on the day of the baptism and the priest had to deal with both the dead and the newborn. The confusion was compounded by a reference to a man who seems to be father and who had just returned from captivity in France, this being 1414.
6. 22/358.
7. For an introduction and useful bibliography, Fione Harris-Stoertz, "Midwives in the Middle Ages? Birth Attendants, 60–1300," in Wendy

J. Turner, et al., *Medicine and the Law in the Middle Ages* (Turnhout: Brepols, 2014) 58–87.

8. 19/996: 19/343: 22/227: 20/842: 18/995: 23/421: 26/464. The midwife was often cited as having been the source of information about the birth: "Emma Kede, 'mydwyfe' met him and told him that William was born" (22/526).

9. 26/464.

10. 23/131.

11. 28/129.

12. 25/129: 22/823: 22/231: 15/891, and also 16/336: 18/990. The presence of men during labor and delivery is discussed, Fiona Harris-Stoertz, "Remembering Birth in the Thirteenth- and Fourteenth-Century England," in Elizabeth Cox et al., *Reconsidering Gender: Time and Memory in Medieval Culture* (Rochester, N.Y.: D. S. Brewer, 2015), 25–59.

13. 22/368. Another juror adds that one Hugh Mortemer "offered mortuary offerings (*oblaciones principals*) for her soul at the church" (of St. Lawrence Jewry).

14. 18/953.

15. 25/524.

16. 22/368: 19/1003: 26/351.

17. 21/876. The inclusion of the wife's father's name is unusual, perhaps in deference to his high status.

18. 17/1110.

19. 18/1123.

20. 22/823.

21. 18/944. The Proof was for Richard LeStraunge and among the participants were the earls of Arundel and of Salisbury, with Elizabeth le Despenser as one of the godmothers. No other Proof refers to such a "multiplicity" and no explanation is offered.

22. 18/855. The Proof was held on 26 January 1403 to verify a birth of 5 January 1382.

23. Joseph H. Lynch, *Godparents and Kinship in Early Medieval Europe* (Princeton: Princeton University Press, 1986).

24. 19/1000.

25. 17/953: 15/65: 18/998: 16/336.

26. 23/309: 15/663, though whether it was canon law or the inability, or unwillingness, to schedule both ceremonies is not clear. Probably the latter.

27. 19/339.

28. 26/146.

29. 26/352. More of this; it might be "2 pewter pots of clarge wine and malmsey wine and 4 silver gobbles," (23/724), or a 'golden awning" for

the church (19/336), or "water from a spring [*de uno forte*] in a small bucket" (26/351).

30. 15/159.
31. 26/147.
32. 20/269.
33. He at least avoided the fate of a more willing godfather but who died six days after the baptism (25/295). The information came from a juror who had been the other godfather and who had attended his fellow's obsequies. This kind of fate—as godparents must often have been quite elderly—may have led one juror to point out that both godfathers, this case, "were still surviving" (15/159).
34. 20/130. That this was the baptism of the son of a peer no doubt raised the social stakes—the prestige of standing as a godparent.
35. 22/527. There is a rare reference to cow's milk but no explanation of why it was needed: 16/196.
36. 23/602. This was the St. Maur heir, in a Proof from Somerset, so the gold coin was not beyond the family's pockets. In another west country Proof the grandmother is quoted as saying to the juror, "'I'm told that your wife is the best nurse in these parts, and so I ask that she be with me, at my hospitality to nurse the daughter to Joan my daughter. I will reward her for her labour and service so that she is well content'" (25/298).
37. 22/526.
38. 18/998.
39. 19/343: 19/665: 25/303: 26/147.
40. 26/156, The baby had been born on 1 September and the nativity of the Virgin was on 8 September, so some stop-gap must have filled in for the week.
41. 18/530: 19/666.
42. 21/149: this was the Proof for John de Holding, brother and heir of Richard, son and heir of John, late earl of Huntington. One trusts that the long-separated couple were well remunerated.
43. 18/664. The juror would have been in his mid-20s when Alice was born, and he was on the scene because he had just "built a new chamber at Elston on 9 September, 1387" and the baby had been baptized on 27 June of that year.
44. 22/223: 21/874: 23/136: 19/899.
45. 26/142: 26/196: 22/678: 24/561: 24/267. One man carrying the kyderkyn "fell and broke his left leg" (17/957).
46. 22/358.
47. 25/298.
48. 22/358. This was the Proof that told of the rejoicing of both Henry Percy and the officiating priest.

49. 21/149. This was the baptism of John de Holand, brother and heir of Richard de Holand, son and heir of John late earl of Huntington.
50. 25/356.
51. 23/139: 24/126.
52. 22/359.
53. 17/430. This is one of the few memories that evoked a try at humor and this might give an insight into the camaraderie of the jurors when they had assembled.
54. 18/1179: 19/344.
55. 19/663.
56. 21/673.
57. 19/777: 18/996: 18/998: 18/854.
58. 19/777.
59. 21/874. The schedule of a rural society and an early start to the day, or just a death coming when it came?
60. 21/874.
61. 26/335: 20/272: 20/131.
62. 22/530: 16/74: "they ate in hall ... on the occasion of the getting up (resurecciione) of the said Fulk's mother."
63. 22/228: 18/996: 18/998.
64. 24/270.
65. 17/1110.
66. 20/272.
67. 19/665: 21/370: 17/1321.
68. 23/311: 24/565.
69. 22/358.
70. 21/871.
71. 26/142.
72. 19/900.
73. 16/398, involving three jurors: 15/652.
74. 15/449. One juror who said he had rendered his accounts claimed that he came away with a surplus of 32s. 6d.
75. 15/659.
76. 24/267: 24/720.
77. 18/677: 22/530.
78. 21/371. One Proof (23/602) tells of 2 different love days. In one, it was one of the godfathers and one John Milborn, with a meeting arranged by friends "to take place after the baptism. Each released the other from all manner of personal action and this was recorded by the parson." In the second, it was the prior of Bath and John Frauncys, who had broken the prior's enclosure and taken game and wood. "They both came to the church on the day of the baptism and with the mediation of William

Cheyne, knight, full agreement was afterwards reached without any money being freed to the knight."
79. 20/263.
80. 15/158: 15/451.
81. 24/560. This inspection of the missal implies that these jurors (all in their 50s or early 60s 1950s or early 1960s) were literate.
82. 18/55, though it was the earl of Warwick in 1361, so perhaps we should accept what we are told. The second case was 18/997, Neville of Raby were the family and this kind of money may really have been handed out at such a time.
83. 20/130. In the same Proof, the juror said he had been given 6s. 8d. from William Bonevyle, but "Eleanor, the mother of his child [the juror's], died on the same day."
84. 23/602. The juror went on to the church where he stayed until "he saw the parson put John's age in a book."
85. 22/825: 15/663.
86. 19/997.
87. 17/275: the juror who "could hardly walk out of the church" because he was so drunk. But unlike many of the memories, in this case he did not fall and break a shin or an arm (20/263).
88. 22/360, 22/361, 22/364, and 23/142 (this last coming from Sussex in 1426). There was a 28-day interval given in a Proof from Braintree, Essex, in 1423 (22/189).
89. 16/1057.
90. 19/158: 19/780: 19/349.
91. 19/341.
92. 22/225: 22/226.
93. 18/978.
94. 19/999.
95. 23/309.
96. 22/824.
97. 23/144.
98. 19/655.

CHAPTER 4

Life in the Village: Good News and Bad

Abstract Most of the jurors' memories related to life in the village—to themselves, to their families, and to others with whom they lived and worked. Their memories often rest on the life milestones—birth, marriage, and death—and these could be offered with some feeling or in the most laconic fashion, touching their children, siblings, spouses, and others whose coming or going left a mark. Beyond the life milestones, there were many recollections of such pedestrian matters as great storms, fires, and accidents, with broken shins and broken arms seemingly quite prevalent among people who did manual labor and who rode unreliable animals. In aggregate these are all memories of what we can consider as the ordinary events—some good, some bad—that reflect the course of life and lived experience.

Keywords Life milestones • Weather • Fire and flood • Accidents and health • Violence and crime

Memories that centered around baptism—the drama that ran from the heir's birth through the churching of the mother—are the most central and, in numerical terms, by far the most common of the various categories of recollection. Of the thousands of jurors who stepped forward and did what was expected of them, those who pegged their recollection on some

J.T. Rosenthal, *Social Memory in Late Medieval England*, The New Middle Ages, https://doi.org/10.1007/978-3-319-69700-0_4

aspect of the drama of a new life being incorporated into the body of Christianity far outnumbered their peers who fell back on a wide range of memories about village life. But from the memories of those who told of something other than the baptism we come away with an array of memories touching many aspects of jurors' lives and activities.

Many of these wide-ranging memories, running into the hundreds if not the thousands, can be thought of as memories of *coincidence*, that is they were memories of things that *happened to happen* around the time of that critical birth or baptism. Some of them involved the jurors themselves, others touched things the jurors had been told about or had seen or just seemed to know about as part of the lore of the community. *In toto* these memories—much like those about birth and baptism—are largely repetitive, reflecting the realities and routines of ordinary life (though with some striking exceptions). We can sort these coincidental memories into several categories: those reporting the milestone of the life cycle, those we offer as tales of "things go wrong," and those that shed light on the status and activities of the jurors as men of affairs. A tally of life cycle memories and of some of the "things go wrong" categories, from four volumes of the *Inquitions* chosen at random, are shown in Table 4.1.

Grouping the relevant memories into categories, we begin with those resting on life-cycle milestones and then move on to "things go wrong."

Table 4.1 Memories of the life cycle, of natural disasters, and of accidents and health

Volume	Number of Proofs	Proofs with a relevant memory	Life cycle events			Hostile nature	Accidents and health	Total memories
			Birth	Marriage	Death			
16 (7–15 R II)	23	19	24	16	18	7	1	66
17 (15–23 R II)	18	17	10	10	20	4	12	56
22 (1422–27)	51	48	42	53	71	34	48	248
23 (1427–32)	49	48	55	48	62	36	43	244
Total	141	132	131	127	171	81	104	

Then we try to reconstruct some daily affairs: the role of the parish church when not being used for the baptism, the social status and civic responsibilities of our jurors, and—in a great panoply of activities—their economic life and secular business, in so far as they fell back on memories of this sort.

* * *

Memories of the life cycle affecting the juror and those of his circle—of birth, copulation (marriage), and death—were often offered at the Proof—as the table indicates. Given that the most useful or convincing of all the memories were those based on the close coincidence of the heir's baptism and that of the birth and baptism of someone in the juror's own family, the large number of such testimonies is to be expected. And, like so many other memories offered, the reasoning here was often circular, the "truth" accepted as offered. The birth-related memories are usually quite straightforward, not much elaboration and only an occasional touch of something out of the ordinary. The basic facts might be all that the juror offered: "His firstborn John was born ... on the same day and he is 21 years and more," giving what was needed with admirable economy and a circularity of logic that never seems to have been questioned. Other terse statements were in much the same vein: "Agnes his wife gave birth to a daughter called Joan still living," which perhaps offers insight into expectations about survival as well as about memory. And while most statements about birth mention that he or she was the juror's firstborn, one juror did tell of the birth of his third son.[1] While these children were well below the status of the heirs, sometimes the baptism of the lesser infant had also been preserved in the written record: "he had a son named Philip born whose age is written in the missal of the chapel." A few birth-memories give us an odd detail. One was of a birth defect, related by a father who said "that day [he] had a son named Richard born without a nose and baptized in the same church," though such problems may have been more common than jurors wished to talk about.[2] A softer touch was a memory of twins. They might be identical, or so it would seem: "his wife was pregnant and was delivered of two boys the day that Elizabeth was baptized." The birth of fraternal twins was also remembered: "Isabel his wife gave birth to twins, a son named Christopher and a daughter named Margery."[3] But sometimes a memory of twins struck a different note, as told by the juror who remembered that "on that day Weburga, then his wife, gave birth to two boys and died instantly after their birth, on which day he came to the church to have the cross and holy water placed and sprinkled on her body."[4]

Memories that hinged on marriage—usually within the juror's own family in some fashion or other—were offered about as often as those relating to a birth (as shown in Table 4.1). However, many of these memories were more expansive, offering a slightly wider glimpse of the lives of the jurors and those about them. Some memories were of that straightforward type that always seemed to suffice: the juror had been "betrothed to his first wife ... and he married her the following Sunday," much along the lines of he "married Margery, who survives," or a recollection that at the key moment he "espoused Alice, still his wife."[5] Of course, that first memory seems to indicate the current presence of a second wife, no doubt something the village would have been well aware of. That circularity of logic that characterizes so many memories continues to show up here: he married Alice, daughter of John Morris ... and that was 21 years ago at All Saints last."[6] A bit of extra family history in one memory: "a certain John Borry uncle of the said Richard, married Margery (the deponent's) sister, and so by the offspring begotten between them he is sure of the age of the heir.[7] Nor are we without references to those written records that established the date also could guarantee the validity of the marriage, were it ever to be called into question: the date had been written in "the great portas of the said church," or, with more detail, we have the memory of the juror who was "staying with John Lyllebon, knight, who married Joan, the date of the marriage was entered in a psalter in Hungerford church and by inspection of that he knows the date." This is much along the lines of the memory of the juror who "married Elizabeth, sister of George de Malton ... on 6 May after the said John's birth and the wedding is noted in the missal."[8]

As was the case with the baptism, the public nature of ceremony and the accompanying rituals and festivities must have helped fix memories. Several men told of the banns having been proclaimed, for all to hear: the rector had "proclaimed the banns between Richard Meysey and Alice" [the juror's sister] or "he married Sibyl his wife and their banns were asked on the day of the baptism."[9] The public and presumably joyous nature of the occasion comes through, as in the joint memory of four men who recalled that "at the time of Thomas's birth they were invited to the wedding of John Pleybury and Joan, who were married the same day." Or it might come from the proud father: "in the week of the birth [of the heir] he married [i.e., he gave in marriage] a daughter of his named Isabel to

Richard atte Kirk ... and gave 40 marks for that marriage." Nor does the beginning a new household, a new domestic unit, go without notice: "he married a certain Felicia ... and took her home to Turvey the same day."[10] But mostly, as we might expect, it was pretty straightforward: "he contracted matrimony with Alice de Whitely, whom he subsequently married."[11]

Though we now accept that most medieval marriages between people of middling status involved men and women well into their years of maturity, some of the marriage-focused memories seem to point to older figures with perhaps one (or both) now marrying for (at least) a second time. The reference to a marriage in the generation above the juror clearly points in this direction: "his step-mother was espoused ... in the church then." Nor was a widow likely to be a blushing bride of 16, as in the memory telling us of when "Thomas Wodye, his kinsman, married Alice widow of Richard Smyth ... and on the same day he [the juror] enfeoffed Thomas and Alice with lands and tenements ... for their lives." Or it might be the juror himself: "he married Agnes late the wife of Henry Makesye on the day" or "he married Gillian previously wife of John Naterell of Salisbury ... and the following 21 March Edmund [the heir] was born."[12] Two memories stand a bit apart from so many of the run-of-the-mill ones. One was a terse recollection: a juror of 54 who offered that "one of his brothers was married that day at Ilkley to a woman of great age." As the juror himself had already been in his 30s at the time of the heir's birth, what was covered by "of great age" is to be wondered at. The other memory that leaves us with an open-ended question, and we wonder if there ever was a mutually satisfactory resolution, comes from a man who had been "with Edmund Brit in the church to arrange for his marriage to Christine, Edmund's daughter, and as they could not conclude owing to her absence [they] arranged to meet the next Sunday in the church," though it must have been at that abortive first meeting when they had witnessed the baptism.[13] Arranging other people's lives is always tricky, as one juror recalled his unsuccessful effort to fix a match, having suggested to a servant of the heir's father "that he marry her but they could not agree."[14]

If memories of marriage were more evocative than those of birth, those taking us back to death and burial spread the narrative even further, though in numbers these memories are about even with those of birth and marriage. Here, perhaps more variety, more variations to the drama, no doubt, and in many cases—judging from the one-liners—such memories were often more poignant, given that they incorporate few happy endings. Some death-memories referred to accidents and a few to various forms of violence. But most, however, seem to look back on death from natural causes (or so we assume when not told to the contrary), though those attributed to mischance or violence or accident do seem to be more memorable. Also, the death of young children or of young siblings or of one's spouse is not hard to call up despite the passing years. There were deaths that followed a long illness and there were others that still stood out for their suddenness. It could be of the latter sort: "Isabel his daughter suddenly died in church" or "John Payn, chaplain and his brother, suddenly died on the day that John Teryngham was born."[15] In the realm of painful memories, it is hard to go beyond the juror who told his tale of woe: he had "married Christine in the church that day and their marriage was celebrated there. After lunch he came to the church to see Philip, father of John, father of Philip, and was present when the parson baptized Philip. When he returned to his house in the same vill at the hour of vespers the same day he found Christine dead. He often recalled this sudden reverse, and thus from the bitterness of his distressed soul (*ex amaritudine anime dolent tordetanus*) he is certain of Philip's age."[16] Long and lingering illnesses were probably much part of home care and the domestic setting, and numerous memories ran back to such: "John his son, whom he loved to hold, died on the Feast of the Nativity," or it might be "his son Edmund, who had been ill for a long time, died and was buried ... on the day of Mary's baptism."[17]

Childbirth, of course, was a time of special danger and some of the death-memories point in that direction. The fear of this particular form of danger must have been all around the folk of town and village, and it is hardly unexpected to find a memory like that offered about when "his wife Margaret died giving birth to a son called William." Bad things happen, and probably with some frequency. But a finger of resentment lingered in one painful memory, the juror asserting that "Alice his wife was in labour ... and for lack of good care over the birth she and the child died." Related to this sort of woe was the memory of when "Juliana his daughter, aged 10 years, was buried ... and Sibyl, his wife was unwell for a long time because of this."[18] Another juror still fell back on a comparable memory: "on that day, for lack of care by her nurse, his daughter named Walkeline suddenly died of thirst in her cradle. For this reason he came to church ... to ask the parson to say divine service for his daughter's soul and saw the parson writing while Philip was baptized ... the memory of his misfortune has never left him."[19] At least one such tale was more mixed, as one died, one survived: "on that day Joan his wife died pregnant of a son Christopher, which Christopher is aged 22 years and more."[20]

Plague claimed its victims, as a juror of 60 recalled "because Joan his daughter died of the plague on the day Philip was born." Another man added to this by noting his son's death from the plague and then went on to offer a hint of a larger perspective, saying that "there was a great plague that year [1408] which killed very many men."[21] Appalling accidents were part of life, as with the recollection that "on that day Reynold his son fell into a well and died and lay there for three days." Danger was on all sides: "his sister was drowned ... in a tank (*cisterna*) called 'malpend,'" and another man had his version of this to satisfy the escheator: he had "lost a son named Robert in a cess pit (*puteus*) in his garden (*orto*)."[22] One juror was hardly likely to forget the horrible occasion when he had "felled an ash tree near his house and the tree fell and killed his son John." Compared to this, a death at sea—"his son John had drowned in the sea near Cromer"—seems easier to live with.[23]

Though the deaths remembered were mostly those of the spouse or a child, we do get a few others: a mother, or an uncle who drowned, or some undesignated relative, and one juror remembered the time when he had "buried his kinswoman, Alice." There was a "grandmother who died on the Sunday after the Annunciation next after the [heir's] birth." To match this, another juror said he had been in church at the critical time because "he had come to bury his grandfather," and it is likely, and more credible, that there were more grandparents in the village than there were 80-year-old jurors.[24] And though daughters figure in these lugubrious ranks, one death among them does stand out; the father remembered the date because "Joan, his daughter, then a nun at Nun Coton, Lincolnshire, died on 22 September, 1402." The detail of the date may indicate that the house had made a special note for a memorial service and perhaps observed its own obit for one its own. Another Proof—one of those theme Proofs on a sober note—not only tells of a memory "because he was at an obit for Katherine his mother on the same day," but it has other jurors at that same Proof telling of the death of a son, of a wife and her obit, of a funeral for a juror's father, of the death of a son who was identified as his father's heir, and finally the memory of one juror who had been "ill and in danger of death from the plague on the same day," though he obviously survived.[25] In a simple tale, one juror offered that "Alice Olney, his mother, died on 20 September 1410 and the following 28 September he had a mass celebrated for her."[26] One memory that proclaims the entanglements of village life is that of three men in a common recollection: "Richard Cobbe, Robert Okys and John Newell, all 49 years and more, say the same and that they know because they were present on that day in the church at the funeral and attended the burial in the churchyard of Margaret, wife of Richard, sister of Robert, and niece of John."[27]

While the references to the death date as a datum entered in a register or service book are not as frequent as other milestones, we do have a few. One juror recalled the date of the birth because "a sister of his died on the day of Mary's birth, and that date was entered in the death register of the friars of Jarum." Some memories are yoked to several of our themes, as with a father who recalled that "his son Robert died about 6 a.m. He went to the church to summon the parson to come and perform Robert's obsequies and saw him baptize John and write his name in a book."[28] The priest had to be adept at multitasking: "Sybil, Churchehull's mother, died on that day and the parson was doing the funeral rites when a man came to where the body lay and called the parson in a loud voice to baptise the son of Christina and John Hulle. He hurried to the church with the parson and the boy was given his name of Nicholas."[29] The services for the dead, along with the funerals themselves, were likely to leave strong memories, judging by what was offered to the escheator. It could be the man who remembered the date because "he was at an obit for Katherine his mother on the same day."[30] But amidst all these sharp memories of pain and loss, we also note that it had all happened some years before and life went on. One form of "life going on" had to do with inheritance and it was hardly shameful to tie this to the memory of death and loss. At its simplest: "his father died and he was his heir." There is perhaps a hint of aggression or defensiveness in one memory: his "father died the same day and his lands descended to him by hereditary right," and even a bit more so with "he might thereby have and enjoy his father's lands and tenement."[31]

Nor did inheritance come as a free lunch: "in the same year Alice his wife was buried in the churchyard ... and the parson there had a red cow by way of mortuary." More of such memories: "his father died. John Hunt, bailiff of the earl marshal, seized a white horse as heriot."[32] As part of the life-goes-on, the dead had, at least on a few occasions, tried to make provision for a future they would not see: two jurors remembered the date of the baptism "because Henry ate Forde died on the day of the birth and appointed them as his executors, and in a peculiar case along these lines,

"John Mayne's wife Ellen, who was sister of William [the juror] was buried at Belvoir Priory. He was her executor."[33] Few references to last rites, though the burial ceremony and the churchyard do get mentioned, and we have one man who had received last rites but who (obviously) had recovered.[34] One juror recalled that "his wife's father died on 31 October of the previous year and was buried in that church. He [the juror] made the tomb."

Only a few memories reach out to the death of an outsider, someone neither an identified relative nor a fellow resident of the village. Ignoring for a moment the execution of various felons, there are but few scattered memories of anyone beyond the familiar circle of village life. A stranger who made a dramatic departure did come in for his moment: "on the same day the exequies of a certain William de Walkeden, slain in the fields of Simundlee in the parish of Glossop, were celebrated, and his death was written in the missal," to give him a formal send-off.[35] In one of the few London Proofs we see the prominence of the city's officials: the juror "knows this because Henry Padyngton, common clerk of the said city, died on the day of her birth."[36] And to end this obituary roll, it is hard to top the common memory of two men, each now 63 years, as they "were servants of Edward III at the time of his death and long before. After the burial [of the king] they returned to their homes at Kenilworth and heard of the birth and baptism."[37]

*   *   *

The memories pegged around "bad things happen" can follow several lines or themes of recollection. Weather-related tales were now being recounted by men who remembered the time of the baptism because it had coincided with weather or hostile nature in a form so extreme that it was still a useable memory. In addition a great many memories were of an injury, usually but not always suffered by the juror himself, with broken shins and broken arms leading the pack in terms of frequency, if not of gravity. In this category we also offer memories related to health—bad health, needless to say (to go along with bad weather)—fever, long-term disabilities, and the like. Finally, "bad things happen" covers quite a few memories of sociopathic behavior of varying degrees of gravity, covering robbery, arson, executions, beatings, knifings, eye gouging, some suicides, and murder. Some of these memories of "bad things happened" are much like the perfunctory ones we have just recounted, a one-liner usually being all that was needed. But in some cases the tales of weather or flood or of being bitten by a dog were told at slightly greater length.

As a general category, the "bad things happen" memories are common, as Table 4.1 indicated. Just to run this down we can look at Volume 23 of the *Inquisitions* (for the years 1427–32), it being a volume with a large number of Proofs. Among the 47 Proofs there are 12 in which at least one juror offered a memory of windstorms and the damage they caused, 15 in which at least one juror talked of fire, 15 Proofs with at least one tale of a broken shin and eight of a broken arm. There are also 16 Proofs with a memory of at least one act of violence or law-breaking or judicial punishment, plus four with memories of health-related issues (other than broken shins and arms). And though that old chestnut of the reliability or veracity of these memories is clearly an issue, nothing was ever questioned or, as the other jurors spoke, contradicted or brushed aside. For weather-related memories it seems reasonable to assert that while memories about the precise timing of extreme weather may be fallible—as any effort at oral history today would bear out—at least one of the forms of extreme weather was likely to have occurred, at least around the right time, and could still be offered.[38] The same degree of latitude about timing may also be applied to those improbably frequent memories of broken shins and arms, given that we have little external evidence that so many of the good men (and a few of the women) of the day went through life with a permanent limp and/or a damaged arm (and we note that whether it was the left or right limb is usually mentioned).

The wind was only an enemy when it was a case of too-much, but such occasions clearly left a mark on jurors' memories. The relevant memories of windstorms are of three sorts, reflecting three degrees of danger. The least threatening was when the wind blew hard but caused no noteworthy damage: "such a wind blew up on the day of the baptism that he and others feared the collapse of their weakened houses," though here the houses presumably had withstood the storm.[39] The next level of threat was wind that really did cause the damage that had been feared: "such a wind blew up in the city [Norwich] that many houses collapsed," or "such a huge storm of wind arose in Haresfield that several men of the vill sustained great damage in the collapse of their trees and houses."[40] Beyond this, as the climax of these memories, there are instances when the windstorm affected life and limb: "there was a strong wind on that day. Dust blew into his left eye at Bigbury by which he lost his sight in it," or "a strong wind on that day threw him to the ground from his horse when he was riding to Exeter, so that he badly wounded (*frigit*) his head."[41] At its most extreme, we have a wind-related death: the juror "swears that such a wind blew up on 8 May 1413 that Richard Ace was blown from the bridge of Sherington into the water, where he drowned. It was said, when the coroner viewed the body on the same day, that John, son of Joan had been born and baptised."[42]

The wind blew as it listeth and, fortunately, not very often. But fire must have been a constant threat, a worry, and a destroyer of property and, at times, of life. While no juror had a tale of anything at the level of the great fire of London, there were many accounts of houses and other buildings going up in flames. The basic memory was a common one, regarding this ubiquitous threat to property and personal safety: he "knows because his house caught fire immediately after the baptism." A few more details were often offered, as when he knew the date "because a windmill was burnt in the night after the birth ... and he and many others saw it," a good fire always being a popular spectator sport.[43] The baptism at issue figured in a more central way for the juror who "knew because his house ... went up in flames. While working to extinguish the fire with his neighbours he saw Ralph carried to the chapel for baptism."[44] We get a double "bad things happen" with the memory of the juror who told of the occasion when "the hue and cry was raised because Benedict Malepas's house was on fire and he [the juror] gathered together with many others to put it out. He fell over a stone in the road and broke his left shin and his right arm."[45] The social side of village life is captured by two intertwined memories: one juror said that his house had caught fire immediately after the baptism, thus his memory, while a fellow juror offered that he had "carried water to extinguish the [same] said fire."[46] Lastly, we can imagine the dismay still conveyed by a common memory of four jurors: "When they returned to Houghton Conquest six days later [from a pilgrimage to Canterbury] they found all their houses and barns in Chapel End there accidently burned down."[47]

After wind and fire we turn to the water-based memories, invariably to be classified in the "bad things happen category." The most laconic of such memories was that of the juror who remembered the time and he "knew because it was raining heavily." Most people had a bit more to say when it was their turn, as with four jurors together: "on the same day the head of the mill-pond at Malsswykesmill was broken by floods," or "on that day the mill of Winderwath was destroyed by the flooding of the River Eden, and it was common talk that Christopher was born."[48]

Grimmer memories in some cases: two jurors had set out "for Lincoln ... and it rained so heavily and the water rose so much that they scarcely avoided being drowned," while—for another memory—it was not even a case of "scarcely avoided" when we hear from the juror who "knew because Thomas his son drowned in the Swale that day."[49] In a Proof at Rutland in 1423 two men talked of the problem of too much water: "John Godard, 58 and more, says that the South Luffenham water mill was broken down and carried away by a great flood that year," and "Robert Palmere, 53 and more, [attests that] that year [he] made a pond (*stagnum*) in his garden (*ortus*) and two of his horses and cow were drowned in it."[50] Closer together in substance, perhaps, are the memories in a Proof held at Lincoln in 1409 when four men are speaking as two separate groups of two: Robert Milne, 50, and John Cole, 43, "had the grass mown from 6 a. of meadow washed away by the flood following the rain that fell that day," and—then from fellows of the same town and in much same vein—William de Kyme and John Hughson, both 50 and more, say "that there was heavy rain on that day, the water overran the banks of the Bain and covered all the grass so that the hay was full of sand."[51] This seems memorable though such a setback hardly ranks high as these tragic tales go.

To this day, recollections of extreme weather help gauge the specifics of the passing years: storm sandy, an epic hurricane, a near-record blizzard or heat spell, and the like. No wonder such happenings were offered at a Proof: "such a great storm in the sea that sea water flooded over the banks of the same vill, almost inundating all the land there."[52] Severe thunder storms were well remembered: "that night there was thunder, lightning, and heavy rain, destroying much corn," and we can try to compare this with a memory of the time when, "about midday a storm of thunder, lightning, and rain knocked men and women to the ground," or, for a painful but individualized memory, "at the time of the baptism there was a great peal of thunder and little boy in the church lost his senses because of its violence."[53] Perhaps we have a juror of unusual sensitivity with the man who recalled that he had "heard such a dreadful thunder that day that he was perturbed in his spirit and badly troubled."[54]

* * *

Nor do these memories ring down the curtain on the bad news. Personal injuries were still something to recall, to enable our men to set the date of that vital coincidence. We have a juror who offered his version of a common memory: he "knows because his horse threw him violently to the ground on the day of the baptism, breaking his right shin."[55] Shins seem to have been particularly vulnerable, with simple falls and slips also taking a toll. Various activities that resulted in this seemingly too-common injury, as the memories go, and we hear of a fair number of shins that had been at risk during football games.[56] Such injuries, or the memory of such injuries, conjure up a world of men and boys sporting on the village green. One man may have been a bit shame-faced when he recalled that he "broke his right leg playing and dancing in his garden."[57] If riding a horse could be hazardous, so was driving a cart along the rough roads, as we are told: he "drove his cart loaded with hay from the demesne meadow to the manor ... He fell from the laden cart in the grange and broke his right arm."[58] One memory straddles the line between a painful event and a possible winner in a tall-tale competition: "there was a great bear-baiting and one of the bears broke the left shin of Richard Mede [the juror's servant]. It was commonly said that John, son of Joan, was born and baptized on that day."[59] As macho memories went, an encounter with a bear probably came out ahead of being trampled by a deer.[60] Other bodily injuries, of varying levels of seriousness, were also remembered. It might just be a simple amplification of the shin or arm tale: "he fell from his horse in a stony lane and broke his right shin whence he has often suffered pain."[61] It may have been a more serious injury: "Richard his brother when working as a plumber on the said church fell to the ground and broke his back," or, if hardly life-threatening but probably quite disabling: he had "served in the hall of Thomas, the father ... and there cut the thumb of his left hand with a knife."[62] If this mishap had occurred indoors, we can go outdoors for another of the same sort: "the juror had badly wounded his right hand killing a boar with a knife."[63]

Life was full of dangers, as the memory of one juror reminded his peers: he "was eating the head of a fish on the day that Gerard was born and almost swallowed its jaw thereby severely injuring his throat."[64] If a broken shin was bad, it was not the only horse-throwing memory: "his bay coloured horse threw him to the ground so violently that four ribs on his left side were broken." Sometimes the horse had to bear the blame: "a surprisingly refractory black horse from which he fell so awkwardly."[65] But to point the finger at one's self was probably more honest: his fall was "because of his haste," and that he "badly injured himself" could not be laid at another's door.[66] Among the tales of falls and slips while dancing or riding a horse, we have memories that take us far from the usual round of woes. At least one man's memory was of a disaster that befell someone else: "his white greyhound named 'Annergh' bit Cadogan, servant of Griffin ap Harry, in the left thigh in the church at the time of the baptism."[67] As we can judge from this terse account, no one seems to have been upset by the presence of a serious dog at church. At least the cat may have been outside, since "on the day that Thomas was born a black cat, standing before him [the juror] ... suddenly attacked his face and totally tore his nose and eyes to pieces with its claws such that he lost his sight."[68] Another tale is of an unusual and painful accident "Alexander Meryng, at the wedding on 13 April, ascending a step below Thomas [the juror] was hit by a spur in the left eye and lost his sight."[69] And in what sounds like an industrial accident, and without workmen's compensation, there is the memory of the juror who "carried such a heavy weight that day that for three days following he was in danger of death."[70] On a less serious note, as injuries go, there is the memory of one who "was at the baptism and played with a player at buckler play (*parmam?*) and there broke his finger."[71]

Alongside the memories of accidents, some of a common nature and some standing out a bit, there are a few recollections of ill-health, confirming the universal dictum that people are happy to talk about their own medical history. We have an interesting but scattered collection of memories, though these reports from laymen hardly take us into serous diagnostics. What "really happened?" we can ask, when "Geoffrey his father was afflicted by paralysis," or a memory of the time when the abbot of Missenden came to act as the baby's godfather but "he had an illness called 'le collyk' and could hardly act," or with the juror who had been "so stricken by fever that he barely survived."[72] Though we say that we forget the memory of pain over time, this folk wisdom clearly bypassed the juror who remembered that "on 18 October 1402 following Gerard's birth [he] had a toothache so bad that he could not possibly forget the pain."[73] The problems of long-term care become vivid with the memory that "on the day that William was born he [the juror] was detained by illness that lasted half a year and more."[74] The most involved of all the health memories was that of a juror at a Proof in Werkworth in 1382. He was clearly eager to tell his tale: "a fortnight before the birth a ruinous stable in which he was standing was blown down by a storm of wind and a beam fell and broke his head almost to the brain. So a fortnight later he came to the leech … to have his head cured and saw the said Mary at the door of the church prepared to undergo the sacrament of baptism."[75]

*   *   *

A final group of "bad things happen" memories relates to recollections of criminal or violent behavior. Some of these woes were inflicted on the jurors, some were perpetrated by the jurors, and quite a few were memories of other people's adventures and misadventures that the jurors knew and were quite pleased to pass along. Most of the violence concerned individual or small-group crimes: a band of three robbers, a fight between two villagers, a stabbing or a knifing and often between parties who knew each other. We can begin with fights and beatings and then raise the level of gravity and move along to robberies and then on to murders, executions, and suicides. Fights, if not uncommon, were sometimes sufficiently memorable, so they marked the passing of the years. In keeping with this, we are not surprised that they could be quite serious, quite violent: "William his son was studying at Salisbury and one of his fellows there in a quarrel between them tore out William's right eye that day."[76] There is something very laconic about the tale of the juror who remembered when the heir's father "hit him on the head with his two-handed sword to part him from his life."[77] No shortage of candidates for this part of the "bad things happen" queue, as with the memory of the day being that on which "Robert, his son, made affray with Nicholas Horton, who struck him and gave him a great wound in the arm."[78] More along these lines: "he knows because in the same year John Sarteler pierced his arm at Lyngfeld with an arrow," or "on the third day after the birth he was struck in the back with a knife by John Casteleyn."[79] Sometimes, at least, it was the arm of the law, albeit after the fact: "Richard Horton,42, on that day struck John Foxley, bailiff of Roger Corbet … on the head with a sword, for which transgression he paid the bailiff 100s."[80] One account of a nasty affair that now may just have been an old memory: "William Dodemour and John de Amerssheton, aged 42 years and more, agree and say that on Saturday after Michaelmas in the same year they fought each other and drew blood from each other, for which they were amerced in the court of the earl of March."[81] One interesting memory tells how words could lead to blows, though we get no idea of what the words were: the juror and a fellow were walking along when—as the juror recalled—"for certain words that he spoke Edmund beat him so that for a long time afterward he despaired of his life."[82]

Violence at the level of people beating each other seems almost commonplace, with the class system exercising some control over who was allowed to beat whom. William Taillour of Tateshale, now 50 years and more, seems to have accepted, as a matter of course, that he had been beaten by Sir Ralph Cromwell, the knight having been a godfather (and then a guardian of his estate during the minority). The juror who had been beaten "remembers because on the day of the birth he was servant and chamberlain of Sir Ralph de Cromwelle, and because he was not present in the chamber on the arrival of Sir Ralph ... [he] struck him on the neck and felled him to the ground."[83] But some of our jurors were of higher status; we have one man who recounted (boasted?) that it was he who had been in a position to beat his servant: "John de Sereby of Lincoln, aged 63 years and more, agrees and says that on the day of the baptism William Hamond, his servant, taking two jars of wine to the church, fell and spilled the wine out of one jar for which ... [he] beat him."[84] While these beatings seem to have been accepted, several jurors did tell of having suffered more severely: one juror, now 59, "was badly beaten and wounded by John Batte at Catton on that day."[85] Again, the effect of the one-liner must cover over a good deal of passion on the part of the man who remembers the baptism, which he "knows because William Astonv and Thomas Reyford attacked and beat him with staves, by which he almost lost his life."[86]

As the jurors offer their memories about anti-social behavior, robbery was the most common of the law-breaking activities they had been involved in, or at least, that they were willing to talk about, imparting the usual degree of sameness to many of their memories. Short and to the point: he had been "captured by thieves at Fringford and stripped of his goods." There might be a few wrinkles on the familiar theme: "One of his servants stole his best horse and fled," and in an even greater affront to the natural order of the world, "he knows because he was in the church when William was baptised and money was taken from his purse."[87] Even the king's highways could be a place of danger: "coming from London on the third day after the birth, with three basins and three pans of bronze that he had bought in the city, and three thieves feloniously took them away," and we might offer that this man had a lucky escape. William Clyfhanger was not so fortunate, as he told of when "John Rake and several strangers ambushed him at Bigbury on that day, in an assault that left him with 3 maimed finders on his right hand."[88]

In one of those "theme proofs" we have three jurors offering separate memories of robbery that affected the community. One recalled that "a thief feloniously stole a grey, good ambling horse from him ... on that day," and the coincidence of his own misfortune and the baptism was a vital part of his testimony. A fellow juror had been "stripped of his horse and harness by three men near Ferry Feyston while riding to Pontefract that day." And their fellow juror had a less personal tale to relate: "the parochial church of Sherburn in Elmet was burgled that day and stripped by thieves of chalice, Bible, and altar cloth," which sounds more like a Viking raid than a tale of the later Middle Ages.[89] Not even traveling with companions was a sure guarantee of safe passage: three jurors in a common memory recalled when "on the Monday before Holy Trinity that same year they were robbed of three horses and 20 marks in money ... on their way to Shrewsbury."[90] And if the roads were no guarantee of good behavior, neither were family bonds: "that month Robert Mostarde, who married Joan his mother [that is, the juror's mother], robbed the nets of William Fienles in the marsh there and took about 60 large eels."[91] But there was some justice in the world, as we see in a Proof taken at Woburn in the 1430s: "on 14 September 1410 a thief was captured at Odell. He broke his shackles and entered the church of Odell and as he leapt at the wall of the churchyard he fell and broke his right arm. The following Sunday Thomas was born."[92]

A few other crimes were mentioned, scattered over the years. One juror remembered when "the king's bailiff, John Balle, arrested Norman Dunstan, esquire, at Harlaxton. Norman was suspected of counterfeiting the king's money and charged to this effect with the multiplication of silver and gold against the statutes." We have no follow-up here but it seems unlikely that Norman had a promising future.[93] In one account the juror seemingly accepts that his son was in the wrong, though the one-liner needs a conclusion: his son was "captured for hunting in the forest of Tonbridge and taken to the county prison."[94] There is one Proof that seems, without corroborating detail, to point to arson: "John Hovell set fire to one of Robert's buildings at Little Dewchurch. John was staying in the same building," which is hardly clarified by the fact that the said Robert was the juror recounting the tale.[95] Only one case (or allegation) of poaching, whatever the popularity of Robin Hood tales: the juror told of another's activity when "a poacher was taken in the park at Beverley and was imprisoned for that cause at Beverly in the same year."[96] One juror evidently fell afoul of the authorities, as he recalled that "on 10 April 1413 at Colchester he was arrested by servants of the vill's bailiffs by virtue of the king's writ to respond to John de Boys in a plea of trespass ... Christine was born on the 23 March before this."[97] Telling of the woes of another may contain one of those few touches of humor, as in the joint memory of two London jurors, recalling that "on the day of her birth Roger Spaygne, 'cook,' was put in the pillory for selling a stinking rib of beef and other unwholesome victuals."[98] And it might be reassuring that in a world of open weapons and quick tempers, we are not entirely without the occasional memory of white-collar crime: our juror himself was the one who had "rendered an account before ... John Hille ... and was found to be in arrears for which they committed him to Exeter gaol."[99]

Murder tops robbery. The simple recollection might be all we have, as when "James Feyes killed William Amell at Great or Little Leighs with a drawn sword that day."[100] As the ultimate criminal act, murder, or the report of a murder, attracted the curious and the memory of such might be embodied in a slightly more elaborate narrative: "that day Nicholas Boister killed John Curteys, Dominican friar, at Salisbury in self-defense near the churchyard. The deceased was seen by Thomas Cuttyng, Henry IV's coroner, and buried in St. Edmund's churchyard the same day."[101] Along the lines of "no good deed goes unpunished," one memory is of the juror's misfortune: "on the same day John Aleyn feloniously killed Robert Buntying at Bumpstead. Richard [the juror] pursued John Aleyn from Bumpstead to Ballingdon and in the churchyard there fell to the ground, breaking three of the ribs in his right side."[102] Another man, doing his civic duty, at least came to no harm: "on that day John Storms was killed by Thomas Dykson ... Dykson fled to the park of Whinfell and Bertram [the juror] pursued him for the felony and was told of the birth."[103] Nor should we omit the one reference to sanctuary, with a juror who remembered that "on that day ... John Williamson was killed by Thomas Dissed, who fled to the church after the felony, and he [the juror] went in pursuit and was told of the baptism."[104]

When the wheels of law did turn, it could be in a swift and draconic fashion: "John Burton, then king's bailiff, arrested Geffrey Normanvyle at Brockst under suspicion of a felony. Geoffrey was taken to the royal gaol at Leicester and afterward hung."[105] As in the Old West of American myth-legend, a horse was a prized commodity and those who played fast and loose with such property were at risk: our juror knows the date "because John atte Stile stole a horse at Dalby for which he was hung."[106] The crime of murder was defined to include self-murder, meaning suicide, and we not only have memories linked to a suicide but indications that it, like a public execution, or a fire, provided a bizarre form of spectator sport. A juror recalled the baptism because it was when "John Hertwode hung himself with a noose at Bosham. He came to see John hanging and, on his return, met a woman carrying John Short to Bosham church for baptism."[107] Even a little more detail in a Proof from Chelmsford, as this time it was to see the man who had "hanged himself from a tie-beam (*laqueo se suspendebat*)." Though with less to offer the viewing public, another suicide memory, but now related in the more laconic style of so many recollections: "at Rockbourne on the day of her birth Thomas Trumpet feloniously committed suicide with a knife worth 1d."[108] For a little variation, one juror knows "because Roberr Bekefeld threw himself from a bridge (*in quodam ponte se imsum emargebat*)."[109]

These recollections that rest on memories of crime (and punishment) pretty much ring down the curtain on the "bad things happen" memories. To conclude with a few memories that were clearly of great importance (and pain) to those who related them, if perhaps not always to their peers and less so to us, there are men who remembered the baptism because it coincided with the loss of valuable farm animals. Years later it still rankled to recall that "the best ox he ever had fell into a ditch and broke its neck."[110] Another tale of misfortune seems to have hit a man of some substance, rather than the juror who told the tale: "a building of Robert Asshefeld, now deceased, called 'carthous,' fell down and a sow with 11 piglets and 5 calves were crushed and killed by the lower door of Asshefeld's mansion ... on the day after the birth."[111] Nor was having 100 ewes dying of a murrain within seven days something to forget.[112]

NOTES

1. 17/594: 23/312: 16:245.
2. 22/226.
3. 22/276: 23/312: another set of twins (16/81) were born on the "Michaelmas day before the birth [of the heir] and their mother was Maud, his wife."
4. 22/530; for a memory that attributed the death of wife/mother to lack of good care, 22/828.
5. 23/139: 22/677: 22/828: 16/107.
6. 15/292.
7. 16/107.
8. 15/891: 19/188: 17/954.
9. 23/716: 15/659.
10. 22/357: 15/159: 15/297.
11. 19/781.
12. 22/359: 17/577: 22/366.
13. 22/362: 19/997.
14. 25/296.
15. 24/275: 23/723.
16. 22/530.

17. 16/81: 21/758.
18. 21/370: 22/828: 23/140.
19. 22/530.
20. 17/955.
21. 24/562: 22/228.
22. 18/672: 15/665: 24/271.
23. 22/222: 18/1181.
24. 19/1004.
25. 24/563.
26. 24/272.
27. 21/558.
28. 15/656: 21/874.
29. 20/272. Churchehull was the first juror and his age is given as 80; he had, presumably, been 59 when his mother died, at which time she too must have been near 80. Of the other jurors, one is aged 89 and another in 80 and more, and both of them, along with most of their fellows, offer a memory revolving around Sybil's death and burial.
30. 24/563.
31. 15/160: 16/77: 19/141.
32. 15/449: 23/142.
33. 16/77: 23/139.
34. 21/875; also, 17/1110 on last rites.
35. 16/336.
36. 17/957.
37. This has to be run down —.
38. C. I. Britton, *A Meteorological Chronology to A.D. 1450* (Meteorological Office, Geophysical Memoirs, no 70: HMSO, London 1937), 136–77. Though Britton combed an immense list of narrative sources, there was no use of record documents from chancery. The extreme weather is listed (p. 177) in terms of "severe winters," "heavy snows," "marine floods," "years with notable wet periods," "years with notable dry periods," and "hot summers."
39. 23/310.
40. 24/398: 25/132: in one case, "the cross of the belfry was blown down by the wind," as four jurors offer in a common memory (16/55).
41. 25/132: 26/143.
42. 24/398.
43. 23/314: 16/341.
44. 23/314.
45. 24/566.
46. 25/475.
47. 18/665.
48. 16/75: 18/675.

49. 18/886: 23/691.
50. 22/222.
51. 19/665. Of the other jurors, four had been in the church for the baptism, one helped put out a fire, one was hurt while leading a bull, and one had been told by the baby's grandfather to give the midwife 20s.
52. 24/721.
53. 19/783: 22/223.
54. 22/825.
55. 24/562.
56. Among many such, 22/187 (broken left shin), 22,360, 22/364. For a memory of having played football without an injury, 21/216. Another juror remembered he had broken his shin while wrestling (18/890).
57. 22/673.
58. 24/125.
59. 24/398.
60. 23/317.
61. 19/777.
62. 15/297: 18/979.
63. 26/468.
64. 22/827.
65. 24/273: 22/673.
66. 24/720.
67. 24/267. There are a number of dog stories: "a mad dog bit him on the shin" (25/521): the juror's "black levrier called 'York' bit Philip" (25/613): a dog bit John's son "in the right shin. Peter [the juror's son] was lamed by this" (23/144).
68. 22/674. It is interesting that a man, blind for 21 years, would be called upon to offer a memory at a Proof.
69. 21/272.
70. 26/588.
71. 19/1000. A buckler is a small shield, as cited in Chaucer, and our juror must have let his finger go beyond its edge when his partner delivered a blow.
72. 23/312: 19/339. In the second Proof there is also a memory of the juror who had "a daughter Joan [who] broke her shin that day," though there are no further details. 23/143: we can add the man who cut his hand "when he was cutting the branches of an ash tree" (26/468).
73. 22/827.
74. 24/719.
75. 15/565.
76. 22/828.
77. 25/613.
78. 26/155.

79. 15/665: 15/891.
80. 15/891.
81. 15/488.
82. 26/352.
83. 17/430. We learn from another juror that Sir Ralph had been "hunting in the chase of Tateshale."
84. 17/576.
85. 25/294. Also, 15/657.
86. 25/303.
87. 23/718, both memories being offered at the same Proof.
88. 25/296.
89. 22/362.
90. 15/448. Another group of three who had traveled together evaluated their lost "good and chattels to the value of £20" (15/894).
91. 19/349.
92. 24/272.
93. 23/139.
94. 25/387.
95. 23/140. A memory of when "Robert Smyth set fire to his smithy" might point to an industrial accident, given name Smyth and craft involved (25/526).
96. 17/1320.
97. 22/830. The juror who was "distrained by 4 hens for arrears of service to the manor of Hurstmounceux parish" got off lightly (15/460).
98. 17/958.
99. 24/124.
100. 22/826.
101. 14/366.
102. 24/566.
103. 18/675.
104. 18/856. A memory of a robber who, while fleeing, "was seen by many people to break his shin bone while running away" (18/316).
105. 23/208.
106. 25/526.
107. 23/142. Alexander Murray, *Suicide in the Middle Ages* (Oxford: Oxford University Press, 1998).
108. 24/268.
109. 25/526. In the same Proof another juror told of a man who "hung himself."
110. 25/387.
111. 19/782.
112. 26/148.

CHAPTER 5

More Scenes from Village Life

Abstract Memories of village events that coincided with that key baptism can be arranged into a number of categories beyond what we saw in Chap. 4. Men talked with pride of having sons (and a few other kinsmen) becoming priests. Some jurors told of having held "public office" at various levels: sometimes in the royal bureaucracy, sometimes at the local level or for the gentry and aristocracy. And, because the jurors were men of good middling standing, there were many memories of their business dealings: buying and selling land, buying and selling animals (sometimes in impressive numbers). Many of these transactions rested upon further references to literacy and written documents: charters, indentures, leases, and the like. The overall picture is one of much activity, mostly being locally focused.

Keywords Social status • Office holding • Ordination • The parish church

Village-based memories that move away from the life cycle and those focusing on "bad things happened" are also numerous and they illuminate other aspects of village life—sometimes daily concerns, sometimes once-and-only moments. We have memories that shed light on the status and socio-economic roles of the jurors: offices they held, officials to whom

© The Author(s) 2018   77
J.T. Rosenthal, *Social Memory in Late Medieval England*, The New
Middle Ages, https://doi.org/10.1007/978-3-319-69700-0_5

they answered, the entry of their sons into the priesthood, the role of the parish church as the center of communal life, and so on. We have many memories that refer to business transactions, usually but not always those of the jurors themselves. As we reconstruct their secular affairs, they bought and sold land and animals, they entered into contracts, they had mixed relations with their fellows, and they offered the usual level of detail about events and doings of 21 years ago.

The jurors could present themselves as the active agents in their memories or, against this, they could pass along their memories as spectators and bystanders. When it was as close a family matter as a memory of a son becoming a priest, it was obviously recounted with pride, as best we can read the simple memory, and whether ordination and first mass really coincided with the exact moment of the baptism or whether it had come within some slightly wider time frame is not an issue of importance. Fellow jurors would have known of such milestones, a son's priestly role being a proclamation of status and, perhaps in some instances, of upward mobility. The village priest not only was in position of power and prestige, but he was on track for what we can think of as a tenured position for life; "local boy makes good" sort of thing. That juror's sons became priests also argues for some respectable level of education and for some sort of training for the duties to meet the standards of the diocese. It is likely that most of these young men who entered the priesthood were already of good middling status and the priesthood was a respected career path rather than a new departure for families on the make. We assume, even for remote villages and impoverished churches, a priest who would come with some modicum of education, perhaps helped out by those popular preaching manuals to help him get through endless round of Sundays, feast days, and fast days. Furthermore, we should note that in the long tally of memories about rituals and sacraments and clerical status, there are never any hints of criticism, let alone of skepticism, concerning the priest's sacerdotal role or the importance of the rituals. Orthodoxy and ritual went hand-in-hand and the king's officials were hardly likely to accept, let alone to record, memories with even the least touch of social criticism. That the baby might be dropped at one or two baptisms, or that someone had to be sent to fetch a laggard priest at the last minute, are interesting vignettes that cover a few isolated incidents. None of the memories show any trace of anti-clericalism.

Some proud juror-fathers put the moment of the new priest's first mass at the very time of the heir's baptism—an instrumental or useful memory, albeit a slightly suspicious one regarding exact timing. But some of these recollections do offer a more elastic coincidence of timing; the ordination came at about the same time, more or less. Whatever the realities of this matter, no one seemed to find anything peculiar about a juror's memory that ran to the effect of "John his son, took holy orders long before that day and celebrated his first mass at Little Laver church the day that Thomas was born and baptised."[1] There must have been a *bona fide* son who was a *bona fide* priest, regardless of the niceties of timing. A few variations on this memory and a little leeway about dates: the juror "had a son ordained in that year who said his first mass in that church about the following 30 November" (the heir having been born on 28 October).[2] Or it might be "Geoffrey his son was ordained [merely as] a deacon that day by the bishop of London," or "on that 28 February 21 years ago, John, son of William Coupland [William being one of three jurors offering this as a joint memory] was promoted to priest's orders at York as appears by this letter shown to them."[3] One of those memories with a circular touch came from a juror concerning the heir who was now 27: "he knows this because John, his son, who was born in the same year as the heir, took priest's orders three years ago."[4]

A few memories of about a priestly role ran to someone other than a son, naming a kinsman who also would have been of much the same social status as the juror himself (and his son): "he had a brother who on the same day that Mary was baptized was inducted and instituted by the ordinary to the rectory of the church of Werkworth."[5] One man's brother had been the "chaplain ... [who] held the book at the door during the baptism."[6] The memory might relate to an uncle, and the identity of a few men imprecisely defined was still close enough to home to be acceptable: "his kinsman ... was clerk of the parish church and celebrated his first mass in the church on that day," or the mass was performed by a kinsman on the "Sunday before Pentecost, 51 Edward III" (in a Proof of 22 Richard II).[7] If memories of these clerical careers and actions were worth offering, there are also a few in which the jurors themselves tell of their own role in the service. Richard Lange, now 55, "was then parish clerk of this church and held the Bible before the priest while John was baptised," or we have one elderly man who still liked to tell that "he knows because he was sacristan of the church and held the book before the priest."[8]

If the memory of a son who became a priest was a bragging point, we note that very few memories steer us to the memories about the education and training that presumably had preceded all these ordinations and (first) masses that were performed by sons, brothers, and other kin. Only an occasional memory about sending a son off to school, though we did note a man who told of his son's serious injury after a fight with schoolmates. A happier outcome, we trust, in a memory of the man who "placed Richard his son in the schools at Cambridge on the Monday following [the baptism], there to study grammar."[9] Sometimes the tale seems a bit tangled, as with the memory of William Howler, who remembers the baptism "because John Roper of Staines, who had three boys, sent for him [William] four days before the birth of Miles and asked if he would provide for one of the boys for three or four years at a school that best pleased him, and William elected Guy, one of the boys, because of John's entreaty."[10] Another memory along these lines reminds us that while our jurors were of good stock, they were far from the top: the juror had sent "William his son to the University of Cambridge with the consent of John Terynyngham [the heir's father] immediately after the birth of John ... [and] John Teryngham gave William 20s."[11] A little forelock tugging here.

* * *

A different window into the status of our jurors is opened when we survey the offices and positions they held, some of obvious importance and responsibility and others of service or dependency. It is only to be expected that our jurors were more than willing to offer that the heir's baptism had been approximate to the time when they had been accepted as the retainer with an annuity, or had been installed in or elected to a position of authority, or had given honorable service to the lord or lady of the manor. Apart from the tangible benefits of such positions, these social and occupational roles might set these jurors apart from their peers. That only a few of the jurors had such memories to offer makes their emphasis on such roles all the more likely. On the other hand there is no indication of any competition or internal contradictions between the 12 memories of a Proof. If one man boosted himself by an elite memory, his fellows must have accepted this as a reasonable response to the question of "how do you remember"?

At the top of our hierarchy of status-proclaiming memories is a juror who said that on the day of the heir's birth, he—Roger Ward, chevalier, 46—"accepted the order of knighthood."[12] No one else ever claimed such an honor and one might wonder how this affected Sir Roger's local standing. But other men did assert that they had held offices of some importance, even reaching the level of minor royal officialdom. One juror told of when he "was elected to the office of one of the king's coroners in the county the day that Henry was baptised," and another, identified as a "clerk," said that he "held the office of king's bailiff in that county" (Surrey).[13] Having been elected seems to have been a matter of pride, regardless of how the election had been held and who had been qualified to vote. Two jurors in a common memory went back to when "they were elected wardens of the gild of St. Katherine the Virgin at Highton by the brethren of the gild."[14] Having been elected constable of the vill of Chepstow in the Welsh Marches or "elected keeper of the prison called 'le Newzate' on 16 January following by the mayor and sheriff of Newcastle" were high points and well worth stating, though how free the nominee in the latter case would have been to decline might be a talking point.[15] Skepticism about the nature of an election seems reasonable regarding the memory of the juror, "elected to the office of coroner on the day that Thomas was baptized."[16]

Without worrying about the method of their selection, we have a handful of jurors who told of their public offices. Though it is slightly ambiguous in wording, it is likely that our juror was probably the constable in question: "he was in the office of constable of Tateshale and arrested John Hunter ... for assaulting and wounding Ralph Eglre."[17] The different roles these men had played, or the offices they held, are interesting for their variety: it might have been while "serving as bailiff in the manor ... [and he] was sent to get Alice Parys to be John's wet-nurse," or the man, testifying at a Proof for an heir to the de la Zouche estates (and title), said that he had been "given the office of parker of Harringworth park by William le Zouche, the father."[18] Brief tales but, as always, sufficient for the purpose: "on the same day he was made constable of the town of Colton," or "he was chamberlain to John de Worsop, clerk, the other godfather."[19] We can imagine how often people in the village must have heard some of these tales: "Roger de Waltham, aged 42 ... says that he was at that time esquire to a certain bishop called 'Saint Nicholasbisschop' and was rewarded with divers gifts to the value of 40d. out of reverence for the said bishop as he served his office, bearing a staff in the bishop's presence."[20] This juror might have had competition from a juror who had been "in the service of the king's bailiff of Colchester in 12 Henry IV, carrying the mace before the bailiffs according to the customs of the vill. At Michaelmas after Christine's birth he withdrew from his office."[21]

This claim (or memory) was bettered by that of John Shadde, he saying that "On the Martinmas 1401 he was made town constable at the court leet held at Salisbury at the great request of the whole community of the vill of Salisbury and, in open court, was sworn to perform the office the following 21 March Edmund was born."[22] One memory fails to clarify whether the juror had been the town crier or the presiding judge: he had "announced in the church on that day [that] the next court to be held for John Knyghtley's manor of Cowley."[23]

Though most of the jurors were below the social level of men involved in the networks we sum up as bastard feudalism, a few did tell of such a world. One juror said he had been "retained with Thomas, then abbot of Pershore to serve him annually as his chamberlain," the knot having been tied around the time of the baptism. We move up the scale a bit with the memory of two men (aged 60 and 52) who on "that day ... were retained for life by Katherine Warbleton, then lady of Sherfield."[24] We continue to climb as we accompany the juror who had been "retained that day by Thomas Sakevyll, knight, for life to serve him in war and peace by a fee of 10 marks. He knows the date by that of the indenture." Nor is this the only reference to our old friend, the written record: the juror had "performed homage to William Lord Roos for a tenement in Belvoir and has a letter of homage."[25] Seemingly below the level of liveried retainers but relevant here, there was the juror who had been "retained as a rent-collector by William Skipwyth, the father [of the heir] and on 6 November last twenty-one years had passed since he was retained."[26] It was worth entering into the record: "Thomas Smyth ... agrees [on the heir's age] because the day Hugh was born he made homage of Thomas Cheworth, knight, for a tenement he held from him in Howton, and thence had a letter of homage."[27] But a fellow juror in a Derbyshire Proof could top this; "John Haweto ... agrees because he was then a bailiff of the king and arrested John Wilman on suspicion of felony and counterfeiting the king's money for which he [Wilman] was afterwards indicted." We are probably coming down the ladder when we learn that "on the Pentecost following the birth of Agnes he [the juror] was retained by the abbot of Dale to serve for one year in the office of donzel," whatever duties fell to a donzel in a monastic household.

Being a servant and admitting such was hardly a serious social come-down as the employers could be assumed to have been people of very respectable standing. Nor were trustworthy servants necessarily kept on the fringes of events, as we find from the memory of the juror who "at the time of the birth he was a servant to John de Coggeschale, knight, grand-father of the said William and went with William de Wauton, knight, to the church."[28] If accompanying one's master or mistress was not unex-pected—he "knows because he was servant to John, prior of Kyrkham, and rode from the priory to Seterington to the baptism"—then being entrusted to help arrange the props for the baptism was even more boast-worthy: he "was a butler of Margery, then Lady Moleyns, lady of the manor, and delivered bread and wine and sent it for the baptism."[29] We have seen the way in which Ralph Cromwell treated a servant when Cromwell's temper was short and menial service deemed inadequate.

Some of the jurors were of sufficient status to have servants of their own. One man spoke in a moving fashion, remembering the date of the baptism because he "had a servant named Henry who died and was buried in the cemetery of the same church on that day," and here the absence of Henry's surname stands out in contrast to the consistent level of detail we find in the Proofs, where virtually everyone—except servants and various criminals mentioned for crime and punishments—is identified by Christian name and surname.[30] A kindlier reference, at least to the level of two names, when the juror "remembered that John Mason, his late servant, was drowned at Romeley in a pit called 'Colepitte'."[31] A final note to a claim to higher status comes from one of the few London Proofs, wherein the juror recalls that the mayor of London had held a common council at the Guildhall, "to which he was summoned but was not present so that he was amerced."[32] Pride at having been expected to be in attendance prob-ably helped mollify the pain of the amercement.

*   *   *

Another way to analyze the status of the jurors is to look at memories about their various business transactions and enterprises. Like the memo-ries of office, the number of such memories is limited, although they are a regular topic of interest, especially because many such transactions rested on a written record. In addition, they touched on such universals as profit and loss, good deals and bad, and good faith and bad. Business activities are quite varied, as we would expect, but we can begin with the jurors who talked of the world of livestock, of the buying and selling of horses, sheep, and cows. This was an agricultural world and both the number of perti-nent memories and the value of the beasts under consideration support the idea that our jurors were men of reasonable substance and, at times, of some initiative with their eye on the cash balance. Against this, as we have already seen, there are those sad tales of bad deals, of uncollectable debts, and of animals that died or went lame rather than living up to expectations and market value. We can begin with simple memories of buying and selling, mostly of larger animals. This was clearly common business and a straightforward memory was clear enough. We have the juror who "sold a white palfrey, on the day of the birth, at Folkingham, for £10 to Henry Beaumont, chevalier, father of John," or "on that same day [the juror] bought a white horse with a black foot for 5 marks," or he had been "at the market at Dudley on that day to buy 4 oxen for his plough," or he had "sold a grey horse for 20 marks."[33] That juror who set out to buy four oxen was either replacing an entire plow team or starting a new one, either alternative being a serious commitment. Some memories along these lines give us a better glimpse of the transaction, a better feel for men doing business: "he sold a horse called 'Skottyshgeldyng Swyft for the Nonys' to John's father Thomas and received payment of £10 for it at the church. He saw the parson write John's age in a book kept in the south part of the chancel."[34] Another of these coincidences of business and baptism: he was "walking with John ate Hull the father, in a field called 'Weryscroft' to look at some oxen which he was buying when a man came to announce the birth."[35] While these memories tell little of profit or loss, one juror seemed to offer a smug memory of a sharp transaction: "on the morrow of the baptism he bought a black horse from William Ryngwode for 10 marks and sold it the next day to Richard Rose for 20 marks."[36]

Big animals and goodly prices could mean a more complicated bill of sale. One man recounted that he had "bought 40 heifers from John Selby for 40 marks, payable at Easter then next following… He then gave John 1d. arrears and 1d. in cash," which leaves us puzzled about how our juror was able to get away with this.[37] In what sounds like the installment plan, two jurors offered a joint memory, recalling the baptism because "on the day Thomas was born they bought a horse called 'Morel Gray' from John Wetewode, his father, for 10 marks English money payable the following Easter. On the same day they made a deed of obligation to this effect and gave it to John who returned it to them upon payment at the agreed date, and they still have it in their custody."[38]

As well as those horse-related injuries that we looked at above as part of "bad things happen," other problems arose around big animals. Though the animals suffered no harm in this case, they were to do our juror little good when "in that same year he was distrained by two oxen by the ministers of John Berners [the heir's father] for arrears of homage and other services."[39] But more animals were lost to nature than to the law: sympathy for the man who "had a white horse worth 6 marks at a pasture in a park pertaining to the manor of Brook. It fell on a pale and died."[40] Though most of the memories take us to horses and cattle, sheep do figure occasionally and but rarely as a source of much joy: he had "met John at Noke driving sheep to Odell and as he drove them over the stream, six were immersed."[41] One Proof, as sometimes happens, seems to have become a sort of oral magnet for related memories—one of those "theme proofs"—about the misfortunes of animals and their owners. In the recollections of a Buckinghamshire jury in 1434 we get numerous tales of woe. The hall at the end of the stable collapsed and the two horses and two cows in the stable were killed. A fellow juror said he had bought 20 quarters of malt but after loading 10 horses with 10 quarters of it, "two of the horses collapsed and suddenly died." Another fellow speaking at the Proof told of when "a great flood in the stream beneath Linford ... [caught] forty of his sheep and they drowned. They were carried by the water to Gayhurst mill and there were pulled out ... on the day of the heir's baptism." Still another man lost 23 of his 40 sheep, "drowned as he drove them beyond the bridge by the mill of Gayhurst" on what clearly should have been a day to avoid that route. The last doleful memory was of when "two of his horses pulling [the cart with timber] were killed."[42]

Other problems stemmed from commercial disagreements, nor were dealings with the clergy necessarily more amicable. Matthew Bysshop had "bargained for a horse that he bought for 40s. on that day ... from Master William Poudstok, rector of Bigbury and the dispute and plea regarding the guarantee of the horse were afterwards long pending."[43] At least another tangled tale seems to have ended on a better note, according to the juror who had sold a palfrey to the heir's father. It was "for £10 legal English money on condition that it proved the best of John's horses. Afterwards that same day, the horses ran about the great close called 'Leypark' near the church and John de Courtenay's horse suddenly fell and injured itself. Nevertheless ... [the father] by his grace gave 40s. to John Russell [the juror] by way of compensation for the devaluing of the horse."[44] Probably more here than we are told and the juror's memory ends on the customary note: while "returning from the close John Russell ... [was] in the church and was present while the parson baptised Philip."

Business dealings revolving around animals are not hard to track. When we come to land transactions—buying, selling, taking on lease, farming—

they are more diverse in nature and with a wider spread regarding the value of the transaction as well as the length or terms of the deal. Furthermore, the memories that revolve around business activities usually provide little hint as to whether what we are being told was a one-off experience or whether it was a routine part of the juror's life and affairs. On the idea that a memory of a land transaction opens a window on social status, we can look at some of the relevant memories, selected from a wide number of laconic tales. In a memory offered by five jurors, they "say that on the same day the said Thomas [third of the five] was enfeoffed by charter of a carucate of land ... and the others were there to bear witness to the seisin, and by the date of the charter they recollect the age of the heir."[45] As we would expect, the mention of the written record is common here: the juror had "bought 20 acres wood at 40s. the acre from the prior of Haverholme. He has an indenture sealed with the common seal of that house," or, for a slight wrinkle, "he had a meadow of land from Richard, the heir's father, in exchange for a parcel of small wood in Wynscore and by the indenture then named he is sure of the age of the heir."[46] Some memories hint at something a bit more tangled, and one at least captures the complications of busy lives: "on Thursday after the Invention of the Holy Cross, 33 Edward III, he purchased to himself and his heirs 6 a. land ... from Thomas Chamberlayn, chamberlain of the said John de Cherleton, and the said Thomas could not come to deliver seisin because of business arising out of the birth."[47] Drawing others into the net as witnesses was not unusual, as with a juror in Devon who "knows because John Gorgeys, father of Joan mother of Joan daughter and heir of John Wybbury, bought a parcel of meadow and land in Chagford from him to give to John Gorgeys and heirs and assigns in fee simple. The charter was sealed in the church of Tormoham in the presence of Robert Cary and others who were trustworthy. He was there when Joan was baptised."[48] Not many jurors indicate that their dealings were conducted with an eye to the future, but we do have one man who in 1413 had "purchased for himself and his heirs two cottages in Colchester from Emma Aldewene, as is clear in the charter made thereon."[49]

Nor were jurors shy about information concerning monetary terms, either for sale or purchase or service. We see this in the memory of a juror who "that day took to farm the manor of Stonor during the minority of Thomas de Stonore [the heir] taking 2d. daily for keeping the park."[50] These flexible arrangements for payment also figure in this memory, though now it was in advance rather than at the next Easter: the juror had "bought a parcel of wood from Henry Vavasour, father of this Henry ... for which he paid £20 sterling in advance to Henry the father."[51] But not always: he "purchased a messuage and 40 acres arable ... for 20 marks, payable on the Easter following."[52]

Other such transactions support the idea that our jurors were men of business, if not necessarily or invariably of great substance. There was the man who "paid £20 for lead on 10 November following in St. Nicolas church in Newcastle, bought from Thomas Langton," our purchaser perhaps being a builder of some substance.[53] A joint or common memory of three jurors went back to when they had "on Tuesday before St. Augustine in the same year they entered into a bond of 100 marks with Richard Toggeford for wool bought from him."[54] One man had been "in church that day and received a windmill at Cowley from John Knyghtley for a 12 year term."[55] And to support Napoleon's jibe about a nation of shopkeepers, there was the man who recalled that he had "a new shop in Colnbrook on that day."[56] An indication of affluence and of being busy men of affairs was offered by a number of memories of shipowners, all telling of a lost vessel and/or its cargo. This certainly sounds serious, as with the two jurors who offered in a common memory: "they had a ship called 'la Trynyte' wrecked and sunk in the port of Cardiff then."[57] An act of nature, we might say, regarding the tale of when "his ship loaded with various merchandise was sunk at sea by a sudden storm the day that John was baptised."[58] It must have been devastating when "his ship, laden with wheat, was ship-wrecked at Hartlepool on the 9 November following."[59] Given the blow these disasters must have been—assuming honest memory about ownership and a share of the loss—the memories are quite contained.

Perhaps he was a man of considerable substance and happy to proclaim it, telling of how he "came that day to talk to the abbot [of Shrewsbury] about his business and saw the baptism."[60] Of course, not all business was conducted along mutually satisfactory lines or in an amicable fashion: he "rode to South Moreton to seek from Robert Brown [the heir's father] 26s. 8d. which he owed him. He said he could not pay him at that time, and a dispute arose between them."[61] One juror, at least, stood as a well-regarded middle man for other people's affairs, as Ellis Beare told when he "was asked to act an attorney for John's grandfather William Bonevyle, knight, in the king's court of record at Westminster to recover certain lands and tenements ... by writ of formedon in the descender against John Petyt of Barnstaple, for which William gave him 100s."[62] At a less exalted level but presumably the memory of an honest tradesman, there was the juror who "was with Stephen the fuller, his father, and that day carried a fulled cloth to the house of Thomas Gilderey and there heard of the birth."[63] And to end on a strange note that reminds us that ownership also means running the risk of loss: the juror who remembered that "there was a sudden fire in which his grange at Winterbourne was burnt. This caused his wife such a fear and suffering that she rode to Salisbury where she was for a long time so ill that her life was despaired of."[64]

*   *   *

Despite what the poet tells us, in this case the center did hold; the center being the parish church, it was the focal point of village life, far beyond just housing or hosting those countless baptisms of interest to us. It stood—year in and year out—as the center of all sorts of social and commercial affairs and, not unrelated to its social role, it was usually the most prominent building of the neighborhood. It was certainly the most prominent one into which the public had easy and regular access. In what is probably a literal sense, all roads seemed to lead to or at least nearby the parish church. This is borne out in such memories as that of two jurors who offered a common memory of having "met neighbors coming from church with Nicholas [the heir] after baptism," or of the two men who "came to the church together to hear mass and met Cristine de Ichene, the mid-wife, carrying Richard to the church."[65] A few memories of this sort are a bit more expansive as the jurors looked back on what must have been a day of general celebration in the village: four men at Penrith "say that Henry was 21 years and more on that feast because they were riding along the high road between Greystoke castle and Threlkend church on the day of Henry's baptism and met various men and women carrying him to the church to be baptized."[66] In a slight variation there were the two men who "met the wife of John Palmer of Bradeston coming from the manor and hurrying home, and she told them of the baptism and that she was with Margery the mother at the birth."[67]

Going back to that idea of baptism as a form of theater, of public ceremonial with all the appropriate rituals and props, we note that it drew spectators well beyond those assigned a specific role. Many jurors simply attested to having seen the baptism; some merely saying they were there and saw it, while others offer a specific reason—other than the baptism—for their presence in the church. The list of "I saw" memories is a long one, though a quick and random dip into these ranks pretty much covers them. Three men together attested that they were "in the church on that Sunday and heard mass and afterwards saw the baptism."[68] This is of interest as it tells something about the agenda in the church that day—the regular service, after which many of the congregation were clearly happy to stick around to see what was an important milestone in village life. Several of these "I was there and I saw" memories come as close to a jocular recollection as we find. One juror remembered that he had seen the godmother raise the baby from the font and then he—the juror—"was present and drank well of red wine and mead."[69] Another juror remembered that he "saw William, late lord Ros, John's god-father with a huge stomach, raise him from the font."[70] Sometimes a particular form of memory seems to have become the memory of the moment, as in a Proof from Lincoln in 1404 with no less than seven jurors falling back on the "I saw" mode of recollection. One man recalled that he had seen Adam, "sometime prior of Sempringham" baptize Henry; another had seen "lady Hawise Luterell, who was the godmother"; a third man "saw Margaret, wife of Geoffrey Cook of Irham carrying Henry to the church"; a fourth "saw Henry carried to the church with four unlighted torches around him"; a fifth "saw Adam, the other godfather, immediately after the baptism, give a little purse of gold"; the sixth "saw four men carrying torches without lights ... and afterwards the torches were carried lighted from the church to the castle"; the seventh "saw Thomas de Bostone, then rector, write the day and place of birth in a great breviary of the church."[71]

Many are those whose memories rested on having seen people who were church-bound for the baptism but who were themselves going there for prayers (though never a mention of confession or penance). A few liturgical details can be winkled out of these memories, with a touch of the ordinary in the memory of a juror who "came to the church with Joan his mother to hear mass on the day of the baptism." At least this stands in contrast to the numerous mother-son memories that look back to her death.[72] Another juror claimed a more active role in church attendance, as he was there, "reading the third morning lesson and [he] heard William crying at the font."[73] We seem to be more in the realm of pious tourism with the four jurors who offered a common memory of when they "came ... to make offering before a picture of the Virgin Mary when the parson was baptizing."[74] When we looked at the bystanders of the baptism we found a few men whose memories went back to their being in the church so they could render their accounts as they finished their term of duty as the churchwardens. One man "was in church and John Tyler of Buckenham sold him a messuage called 'Godalys' in Buckenham," which calls to mind the money-changers whom Christ drove from the temple.[75] Along this line, there was a memory of three jurors: "present in the church and John, then receiver of the sheriff of Berkshire, received from Thomas and Thomas [two of the three men offering a joint memory] 10s. 8d. of their issues, forfeited in the King's bench and exchequer."[76] No indication of any embarrassment in recalling this transaction, and it reminds us of the thin line, at best, between the church as a place of prayer and as a de facto village hall: "John atte Forde, 50 and more, came to the church on the day she was born and sued a bill against Thomas, Lord Scales, Eleanor's grand-father, at the time of the baptism."[77] Rendering the accounts was obvi-ously a serious matter in a world where the laity were responsible for the physical upkeep of the church, and two jurors told of the day when they "rendered account of goods, etc., bequeathed to St. Mary in the parish of Whitchirche at divers times, as is enrolled in the missal thereof."[78] But the parish church was also under the eye of the ecclesiastical hierarchy, as made clear in a memory of a time when the dean of Norwich came and "caused to be enrolled there all the ornaments of the church, which enrollment was noted in the processional (*precessionario*)."[79] More in keeping with the idea of the church as the center of village life and a logical and convenient rendezvous point, a Proof with a memory common from all 12 men says that "they were there in a company as pilgrims and saw ... the heir's god-father lifted him from the sacred font."[80]

When we looked at the baptismal drama we noted some men who said they had come to church to be involved in the resolution of a quarrel, that is, for a loveday and that their presence just happened, once more, to coin-cide with the baptism. Certainly, resolving a quarrel, in church and espe-cially through the agency of the priest, was indeed a good way to have closure: the right place and the right person. So whether medieval society was especially quarrelsome or whether our jurors' memories were intended to highlight an irenic way of resolving disputes, depositions that focus on the details of lovedays are offered from time to time. The common mem-ory of five Londoners is a little ambiguous on this: "they were at church with John Walleworth, then mayor, for an inquisition between the prior of Elsing Spital and Walter Doget, then sheriff."[81] Another memory along these lines, clear if laconic: the baptism had been "about the hour of ves-pers. They know because they were at Honiton for a loveday," as three jurors said in a common memory.[82] Another local quarrel seems to have been resolved to mutual satisfaction: "this was recorded by the parson."[83] But sometimes, perhaps because it was a dramatic event and the jurors were proud to have played a role, though perhaps only as spectators or witnesses, we get an unusual amount of circumstantial information. Five men of Bristol knew the heir was "aged 21 years and more ... because during his baptism they were in the crypt of the church when an agreement was made between Richard Gargrave, 'bowyer,' and Thomas Clyve, 'goldsmyth,' following a long dispute between them. A day for reconciliation had been appointed and an arbiter for each chosen at the instigation of John Somerwell, then mayor of Bristol. After agreement was reached between the parties, they came before the mayor and John Castell in the church after John's baptism and had the arbitration enrolled, and because John Somerwell was mayor of Bristol in 1393–4, the deponents know that John Solers is aged 21."[84] A comparable memory was offered by four jurors at Bedford, they now remembering because "before his baptism they arbitrated in the church in a certain cause between the abbess of Elstow and the prior of Cauldwell concerning the tithes of a field called 'le Ha' and saw an agreement made and recorded in a missal belonging to the church."[85]

* * *

In addition to the many activities that were housed in the parish church—some integral to its sacerdotal functions, some to its social ones—there are those memories that center around the church itself as a building. These bespeak a concern for the structure; the need for repairs, the acquisition of new ecclesiastical items, and a community involvement in its upkeep. We can begin with memories focusing on the outside of the building, some taking us back to those "bad things happen," as in those purported windstorms that swept the kingdom. It might seem as though the parish church could have been built in a sturdier fashion, perhaps with a less ambitious belfry. A lasting memory: "the bell tower of the chapel was blown down by a high wind," or the juror "knows because there was such a great wind that the belfry of North Cadeby fell to the ground," or "an ash tree from the west side of the church fell on the belfry that day."[86] And in what seems like a gift of thanksgiving, two jurors recalled that: "after vespers on the day of John's birth Thomas [John's father] gave 40s. for the repair of the belfry."[87]

New construction must have been gratifying and here too, memories helped put a bright face on many a parish church. One memory gives some unusual details: "Thomas Axe [the juror] ... was in the church to receive 20 marks from the parishioners in payment for building a new roof for the church and also received 13s. 4d. for himself," though the profit margin seems suspiciously low.[88] A juror in Chelmsford "remembered the day because a new bell was then hung at Downham church."[89] In a Proof in which the churchwardens told of rendering their accounts, fellow jurors told of a new roof for the church at Sawbridgeworth and that it was also the time when "the great bell of the church ... was bought."[90] Beyond just the memory of a new bell, there was the recollection of one man who knew the heir's age "because that day he and other neighbours bought the great bell of the church called 'sweetmaria of Shorehoge' parish St. Benet," in a London proof.[91] Construction sites are always popular viewing stands and several memories talk of this popular form of voyeurism: three jurors recalled that they "were standing in the churchyard and looking at masons who were building the church when Elizabeth was baptized," or from a juror who "was at Bosham to see the timber cross for the church belfry."[92] Finally, before we move inside the church, there was that churchyard, as four men remembered in a joint memory of when "on the same day they began to erect a stone cross in the churchyard."[93]

More memories as we enter the church. Sometimes the jurors were just spectators, as was the case with a man who remembered when another parishioner "had a window placed in the church of Woodhay in which the date is written," or they (two jurors) "were present on the said day and the parish of Sutton began to make two altars in the body of the church."[94] In other memories, the juror himself had played a more active role: the juror had been in the church to make "a footstool [*scabellum*] before the altar of the Virgin Mary at the time of the baptism."[95] In one of the few memories that point us to the spiritual side of church life, a juror in Warwick in 1401 said he "had a wooden cross made and raised in the church on that day in honour of the Trinity and for the health of his soul."[96] Four men had made "a contract with a carpenter called John Gylmyn for repairing a chantry in the church called 'Chelrey chantry' and they saw the baptism."[97]

Of different sorts are other memories of the church: gifts, decorations, books, and some odd touches of peculiar events across the years. We can go back to the mnemonic power of the book, that precious artifact, into which so many of those baptismal dates had been entered. In some cases, as the jurors guide us to the book, three men told of how on the day of the baptism, "the parishioners there decided to buy a missal with the goods the said Thomas [father of the heir] bequeathed to the church and a month later bought the book."[98] Another juror offered one of those memories that call for a bit more amplification: "on that day he brought two books, one of which was a missal, to the said church, and sold them to the said John, one of the god-fathers."[99] In what sounds more like a community contribution, we have the memory of when the two proctors of the church "delivered a missal to the rector in the presence of the parishioners, to remain in the church for use in perpetuity."[100] New items to replace old ones, though it was not always normal wear-and-tear, as we learn from five men of Derby, "each aged 62 years and more ... [and they] say that they were there on the same day and bought a missal from the parishioners of Sutton and gave it to the church of del Heth because the missal of that church had been stolen." The parish church at Sutton was clearly getting a bit of a makeover, since four other jurors in that same Proof had "entered into a bond for 100s. with the parishioners of ... Sutton in Dal, on behalf of Thomas Mason, that the said Thomas would well and faithfully enclose the churchyard of the church of Sutton."[101] New construction and gifts were always on the wish list, gratified in one case according to a recollection of when "William [lord Bonevyle, the heir's father] gave £20 to the fabric of the church."[102] It seems unlikely that the juror who offers this tale of a gift is speaking about himself when he says that "about Easter of that year, 1384, the patron of the church of Weaverthorpe and of the chapel of West Lutton gave a whole vestment of green silk for the souls of his late father and mother."[103]

There are also occasional memories of incidents and odd happenings centering around the parish church. One memory reinforces the idea of the parish church as the village hall, as when a juror recalled how he "rang the bells discordantly (*pulsant campana contrarie*) in the church belfry because of the fire at William Wright's house."[104] And in a memory that seems well out of the usual loop, it was in St. Benet Sherehog in London that "William Colecok and Isabel, his wife, Richad's sister [he the juror of memory] were divorced."[105]

To close on a sanguine note and positing a world in which there was no need for lovedays or forgiveness and in which all baptized babies (and their mothers) would live long and satisfying lives. Wrongs could be righted, as we have seen, and pollution could be washed clean. We have the memory of Thomas Martyn, given on 23 April 1384, telling us that "the church of Weaverthorpe, of which the chapel is a member, was polluted by blood shed between John Webbe and William Belle of Weaverthorpe and was re-consecrated by the suffragan of Alexander Nevyll, archbishop of York, on the day of the birth."[106] With less detail but still offering the basic information, there is the juror who knows the date of the baptism "because the altar of St. John the Baptist in the church was consecrated the same day." Likewise, and with no reason given, "on the same day the church of Bilburgh was dedicated anew."[107] Finally, with both a touch of nostalgia and sociability, we have the testimony of 12 of our jurors, "each aged 50 years and more" and obviously enjoying their tale: "This they know because the said church is dedicated in honor of St. Valentine, on whose feast day there is a small fair there, and several of them were there on account of the fair and saw John Hautlo and Thomas Baa, grandfathers of the said John, lift him from the sacred font."[108] The collective memory of old friends, bespeaking a day off from work to go to the fair and two living grandfathers on the scene to welcome the baby. A good stopping place on which to leave village memories and to turn to what we can learn about the world beyond those narrow bounds.

NOTES

1. 22/360.
2. 18/1180.
3. 24/128: 18/857.
4. 16/107. From another juror at the same Proof, we learn of "a mighty wind through England 23 years ago, at which time the heir was 3 years of age and more and recognized as such by his kinsmen, acquaintances, and friends."
5. 15/656.
6. 24/400.
7. 21/875: 17/1319.
8. 22/527: 24/562, and Henry Wygge was now "65 and more."
9. 25/351.
10. 25/303.
11. 23/723.
12. 23/309. The Proof was that of William Ingilby son of Eleanor, daughter of William Moubray and Margaret, she having been wife of William Cheyne, chevalier.
13. 22/831; 23/718.
14. 15/449.
15. 23/423; 25/295.
16. 23/724.
17. 17/430. This is the same Proof as that in which several servants of Lord Cromwell remember that he had beaten them for various transgressions.

18. 22/678; 22/562.
19. 15/893; 17/576.
20. 15/159. The Proof was held at Leicester, the Wednesday after St. Peter in Cathedra 2 Richard II. The Proof was that of William, son of William Deyncourt, knight.
21. 22/829. The chances are that he was dismissed.
22. 22/366.
23. 20/671.
24. 22/674; 18/990.
25. 20/265; 23/139. For the same statement of homage, this time to Lord Beaumont, 23/308.
26. 23/419.
27. 24/567.
28. 15/291.
29. 16/954; 18/1123, this being a Proof of Age for John Arundel in 1406 and obviously a ceremony that drew some peers and their ladies.
30. 25/336.
31. 26/245, though little difference it would have made to Mason.
32. 17/1321.
33. 23/601: 26/145: 18/994: 19/342.
34. 21/874.
35. 20/272.
36. 19/999. Neither of these other men is otherwise mentioned.
37. 23/596.
38. 24/560. One man bought a horse for 100s and also gave his bond to pay by or at the following Easter: 19/781.
39. 15/657.
40. 26/352.
41. 24/272. The sheep may have belonged to the John whom the juror met, but regardless of who owned them, they were dead.
42. 24/398. This Proof takes on a "can you top this" style, with memories of a juror who broke his shin at a bear baiting, a man blown off the bridge and drowned, a man who almost drowned when "his horse staggered and fell," another broken shin from a fall while fighting a fire, and finally—3 broken ribs on the right side from falling while pursuing a felon. At least one man could offer that his daughter had been confirmed by a suffrage bishop on the day of the baptism.
43. 25/296.
44. 22/530.
45. 15/655.
46. 23/139: 16/107.
47. 15/659.

48. 25/298.
49. 22/830. A fellow juror said he had on that day "purchased to himself and his heirs 8 a. lying in Colchester ... as in clear in the charter made therein."
50. 20/265.
51. 22/262.
52. 23/140.
53. 25/295.
54. 25/448.
55. 21/671.
56. 16/1123.
57. 20/184.
58. 22/677. More "bad things happen" about ships are offered: "lost a ship in a sudden storm at sea" (23/141).
59. 25/295.
60. 21/1148.
61. 26/354.
62. 21/874. A fellow juror said that "on that day John's grandfather, William Bonevyle, knight, acquired a piece of meadow in Pen from him to hold in fee simple by a charter sealed in the church of Pen."
63. 22/350.
64. 22/828. This sounds like what we would think of as "a nervous breakdown."
65. 19/392: 19/999.
66. 21/368.
67. 18/996.
68. 18/129.
69. 15/613. The mention of the two forms of alcohol probably means that they were usually beyond his own purse.
70. 23/601. This juror's memory is about as close to a sarcastic or critical comment system we have, whereas the beating of a servant (by Lord Cromwell) was a normal part of social hierarchy and it seemingly was so accepted by the servant (17/430).
71. 18/998. Other jurors had held torches, had heard a discussion about the choice of a name for young Henry, told of rabbits being sent for the post-baptismal dinner, discussed the choice of a good wet nurse with the mid-wife, named the godfather, and told of a gift of a silver cup.
72. 19/99.
73. 18/673.
74. 19/777. A similar goal drew jurors to a picture of St. Leonard (19/778) and St. George (19/786). Either there was an outburst of iconographic art or this kind of memory was a respectable one to offer.
75. 21/673.
76. 21/146.

77. 25/527.
78. 15/449. That the missal, rather than account rolls, was the proper place for such an inventory is of interest.
79. 16/1053.
80. 15/654.
81. 19/141.
82. 20/130.
83. 23/602.
84. 21/371.
85. 21/558. Interesting that the record was set down in a service book of the church when both parties were regular clerics and presumably represented houses that kept their own records, probably in addition to what our jurors were concerned with.
86. 18/675: 25/526: 20/844.
87. 21/874.
88. 20/269.
89. 20/841.
90. 25/525.
91. 26/148. The only other urban-focused memory was from a fellow juror; "the altar of St. John the Baptist in the church was consecrated on the same day."
92. 23/137: 23/142.
93. 16/76.
94. 19/188: 15/892.
95. 18/999.
96. 18/667.
97. 20/268. The maternal grandfather of the heir was a Chelrey and, no doubt, had founded the chantry and made the original endowment.
98. 15/652. It sounds as though someone was given the money and authorized to go shopping.
99. 17/576.
100. 23/716.
101. 15/892. It was also the day on which the parishioners began to make two altars "in the body of the church."
102. 20/131.
103. 19/341.
104. 25/475.
105. 20/148. This is the only memory of such a proceeding—an annulment, perhaps?
106. 19/341.
107. 15/893.
108. 15/658.

CHAPTER 6

Life Beyond the Village

Abstract In the course of their lives many jurors had memories of events, their own doings, or things of passing interest that looked beyond the usual boundaries of village life. Several sets of memories centered on activities that led to a new life style, whether in or near the village, in a physical sense, or elsewhere in the realm. These were putting a son into an apprenticeship and having a relative, male or female, enter a house of regular religion or a friary. Another activity that by definition went beyond the village and that left a lasting impression was pilgrimage, and it might be just telling the fate of another who had done so. In addition, the dangers of war were often present, and a raid by the French or Scots, or the passing of Owen Glendower's army—sacking the town, taking prisoners, being resisted as the king's army passed by—were things that stayed fresh in the memory and were not infrequently offered at the Proof.

Keywords Pilgrimage • Apprenticeships • Monastic vows • War and foreign enemies

Our vast pool of jurors was comprised of men who, with their families and neighbors, lived most of their lives within the rough boundaries of their village or community. But they were also men of some substance and probably of some sophistication about the wider world and, accordingly,

© The Author(s) 2018
J.T. Rosenthal, *Social Memory in Late Medieval England*, The New Middle Ages, https://doi.org/10.1007/978-3-319-69700-0_6

they would sometimes offer memories about extra-mural experiences, that is, experiences and events that look beyond the usual parochial boundaries. These memories are clustered here into four categories: memories (and testimony) regarding pilgrimages, those touching regular religion and regular houses, those dealing with apprenticeships, and those that offer a view of foreign and national affairs in some sense or other. References to pilgrimages are self-explanatory. For regular religion, we work on the idea that when a man or woman took the vows of monastic or mendicant life, she or he was leaving the world of the social village and of secular society, regardless of the actual location of the house. A memory that centers on an apprenticeship, usually one focusing on the placing of the juror's son, also seemed to mark a move outward if not necessarily upward. Like the entry into regular life, regardless of location, the new apprentice was usually embarking on a future that was not a direct father-son legacy. Lastly, a medley of memories about the outside world ran from those telling of a personal involvement, such as military service under Prince Hal, to recalling the critical year (of the heir's baptism) by its coincidence with the Peasants' Rebellion or the sighting of a comet.

Pilgrimages, by definition—unless one happened to live within walking distance of Thomas's shrine at Canterbury—were an extra-mural experience, one that took the pilgrim (or pilgrims—joint journeys seemingly being quite common) beyond village boundaries. A memory of going on pilgrimage figured across the years and the long-life of such memories marks them as something well out of the ordinary run of life. It also confirms that many of the jurors were of sufficient substance and had free time to travel to the outer bounds of Christendom.

Table 6.1 shows pilgrimage as an activity that engaged a modest number of jurors but that proved to be of enduring interest over the years. An early tilt toward Santiago as the destination of choice yielded over time to a greater interest in local sites: not just Canterbury but York, Bridlington, and some undesignated place only named as St. Margaret's.[1] Most of the pilgrimage memories are simple enough and a few tell of the pilgrimage of someone other than the juror himself. Also, we note that what is offered as the memory is more likely to be dated in terms of the date of departure, fewer references to the day of return. One man did offer that his father "set out on his journey to the Promised Land on that day," and three men, in a common memory, recalled that "they were journeying on pilgrimage to St. Thomas of Canterbury and during their pilgrimage they were told in London of the birth of the said heir by Robert de Hoo, the heir's

Table 6.1   Memories of pilgrimage

Volume of IPM	To Jerusalem	To Rome[a]	To Santiago	In England[b]	Total
15	2		4	3	9
16			3	1	4
17	1	1	1	2	5
18		2		2	4
19	4	2	1	2	9
20	1				1
21	1	1			2
22				2	2
23	2	2	1	1	6
24				1	1
25		1		3	4
26					0
Total	11	9	10	17	47

[a]Reference is sometimes to "The Court of Rome" but a pilgrimage, rather business at the papal curia, is assumed

[b]As well as Canterbury, York, Bridlington, and an unspecified "St Margaret's" are named. No mention of Walsingham or Bromholm or of any local shrines

god-father."[2] When it was the return, as it had been for two jurors and "two other chaplains," the memory might offer a bit more information: they "came to Stowlangtoft from the Holy Land and the court of Rome and brought Robert Asshefeld, now deceased, a 'quinquinnale' for himself."[3] In one case the return from a domestic journey did leave a lasting impression: "on his way to Canterbury ... and it was commonly said as he returned home through Chiselhampton that Philip had been born and baptised."[4] Some jurors state that the pilgrimage was to honor a vow: "in accord with a vow that he had made," or—in more detail and coming from two men—"on Thursday before All Saints in the same year [as the baptism] they set out together for Santiago in accordance with an oath which they jointly took when in peril of water."[5]

The long journey carried obvious hazards, and whatever the cause of the deaths, several memories are of pilgrims a father and a brother—who left but who did not return: "Robert Stok his father, in the same year started on a pilgrimage to the Holy Land where he died," and "on the morrow of the baptism John his brother set out for the holy Land and died on the journey."[6] As we know from pilgrims' accounts, people often made these journeys in a group, or at least with some companions, and jurors' memories accord with this: the juror who "was on a pilgrimage to

Canterbury with Fulk's father when his mother was pregnant and gave birth," perhaps an insight into the father's priorities (though he may have gone to pray for a safe delivery). In one joint memory, two brothers tell that a third brother had gone to the Holy Land, though he too died somewhere along the way.[7] But some of the memories touching this aspect of popular religion, remind us of the realities of travel, and one rather droll and chatty memory weaves a number of themes: the juror "knows because Isabel wife of John Roudon sent for him as she had frequently done before … He came … and met her in the churchyard. She wanted to buy his grey horse to ride on pilgrimage to the priory of Bridlington. William sold her the horse for 10 marks 6s 8d., paid there and then, and [he] subsequently entered the church where he saw the parson writing John's age in a certain great book. The horse was the best and most sure-footed he had ever ridden."[8]

Another category of out-of-village memories are those that relate to some aspect or other of regular religion. It was usually a memory of when a son or a daughter had gone through these one-way gates, though occasionally it was something that concerned someone else or even some doings of or within the house itself and without any stated personal link. The timely coincidence of heir's baptism and a juror's child turning his or her back on the world was a memory offered from time to time, as when his "son John was ordained a monk in the abbey of Malmesbury on that day, and this was recorded in the chapter book of the abbey," or "his son assumed the religious habit in the house of the Carthusian order in London."[9] A reference to the life choice of another could also be the mnemonic of choice, as for the man who recalled when his brother had been "made a monk in the priory of Wenlock on Monday after St. James," while another told of an undesignated "kinsman (*congnatus*) of his named Richard [who] assumed the religious habit of the monks of the order of St. Benedict at Wenlock."[10] Jurors had daughters as well as sons: "in the same year his daughter Katherine became a nun in the house of Katesby and was professed there," while we noted above the sober memory of "Joan his daughter then a nun at Nun Coton, Lincolnshire, died on 22 September 1402."[11] And among the sons, it might be induction as a canon rather than as a monk, still a source of pride (and counted here as under the penumbra of regular religion). Two men offered a joint memory, as "they had two sons made canons in the Abbey of Houghton as is noted in a certain book in the abbey."[12] We hear even more paternal pride in the memory of the juror who "swears that on the Wednesday after the Sunday of Philip's birth John his first born son was elected canon to the Benedictine monastery of Dorchester."[13] Furthermore, against views of declining appeal of the mendicants after the Black Death, we find sons who chose this as their pathway through life and whose choices were remembered by their fathers. One juror recalled that it was "within fifteen days of that date his eldest son took the habit of the friars minor in Babwell," and a juror in the southwest said that his son "was professed as a Franciscan friar in the friar's convent at Exeter the same day that Christine was baptized."[14]

The date of a child's entry into a regular house was a reasonable way to fix the year. Sometimes it was more than a memory of taking vows and entering the house; we have those that look at the rhythms and operations of regular life, as we see in a brother's recalling that "on the same day Agnes his sister was elected prioress of the nuns of Arthyngton."[15] An aunt had been elected a prioress and a brother-in-law's elevation elicited a more detailed account: "Thomas Stotesbury esquire, 63 years and more, rode with his brother John Stotesbury, to Chalcombe abbey to see his wife's brother Thomas Blysworth, one of the canons, made abbot on 12 February 1400."[16] But it might be of the younger generation, as when "John his son was elected abbot of Pipewell."[17]

Personal memories are only to be expected. Also of interest, however, are some that peg the juror's dating against an event in a regular house but one that did not touch his own kith and kin. Presumably, what went on in a nearby monastery was of local interest and much gossip probably circulated during a time of transition, let alone when there was a scandal or an episcopal visitation. There is no stated personal link between the juror and the subject of his memory: "that day John Winthorp, abbot of Hagnaby, was elected abbot of that abbey."[18] Nor is there any obvious reason for the memory of Henry Bagshot at a Proof in Kent in 1417: "Agnes Bongesett, prioress of St Hames's hospital, Canterbury, died that year. Lacy Clemency prioress from the death of Agnes has been so since the death of Agnes, for 21 years."[19]

Another group of memories that take us beyond life in the village are those that talk of apprenticeships. It was usually a case of a juror recalling when he had made a contract to have his son so treated and trained, though in a few instances it was an autobiographical memory. Usually the memory ran along the lines of recalling when he had "apprenticed John his son to Richard Bakere at Cambridge to learn the art of bakery," though it might be when his father had "caused him to be apprenticed ... in the trade of a saddler by a covenant contained in certain indentures."[20] As we said above, even if the apprentice served his time in his father's village, setting him on this road was a new departure. The contracts were for seven, eight, or ten years, and none of the relevant memories ever give any sort of follow-up information, 21 years later, about what happened when the stipulated years had passed.

Though the memories are, once more, fairly standard in both wording and content, we find an impressive variety of different trades, skills, and crafts, all ready and able to accept the sons and turn them into the journeymen and perhaps the masters of the next generation. Young men were sent to learn the mysteries of saddlers, butchers, carpenters, weavers, grocers, drapers, leather dressers, merchants and mercers, "wolman," "peutrer" (pewterers), tailors, and bakers.[21] The point of the training was obvious: "to learn the art...," "to learn the trade and to serve him...," or "to learn the art of bakery." Though it was always understood, not many of the memories were explicit about the *in loco parentis* aspect of the arrangement: "placed Richard his son with Robert Samford of London, draper, to serve Robert faithfully as a live-in apprentice for ten years."[22] A few of the memories reveal a more complicated arrangement, or one with an element of reciprocity—the son in training and the father coming in for a share of the master's profits: the juror apprenticed Henry his son to William Swandon of Colchester, 'peutrer.' "He delivered 10 marks in money to William to invest in merchandise and then to release half of the profits at the end of the year."[23] Nor was this a unique arrangement, for another juror recalled that he had "handed over £10 in cash, with half the resulting profits to be paid to John Smyth [the juror and the apprentice's father] at the end of the year."[24] And without any mention of sharing the profits, one father "apprenticed his son to a 'wolman' of Grantham and before an alderman and others, delivered £20 to Thomas [the wolman] for his son's use."[25] As suggested by other memories, the world of the jurors was one of men of reasonable means, willing—at least in some instances—to invest in their children's futures. It is hard to know how to classify the apprenticeship of a juror who had been sent to one John Wylegh, "one of the receivers of the issues of the vill of Chichester."[26] And in a different vein but also a form of training and a reference that makes education sound like a form of training, we have a juror who "put John, this first born son, to school at Great Hollingbury."[27]

The last group of memories that we offer as "life beyond the village" are a mixed bag of recollections—some personal, some merely references to events that took place around that time, or that happened to others but were known to the jurors. One theme that runs through many of these memories is that the kingdom was often at war: the Scottish borders, the marches of Wales, the coasts that were open to French raiders. Some of our village men were caught up in such affairs, and often hurt by them, and with little choice in such matters. Others could tell of adventures and experiences that probably set them off from their more domestic fellows, whether they came back as winners or not.

Personal memories were the most vivid and they often link our villagers to "larger" events. One man was on Bishop Despenser's dubious "crusade" to the Low Countries: "he remembers because on that day he was retained by the Bishop of Norwich to accompany him on his voyage to Flanders," an experience that at least might get our juror a footnote in the history books.[28] A more glorious military adventure was recalled, probably after endless retellings in the village, as one man remembered the baptism "because the same year that Margaret was born, he came with Henry V in his third year as King from Normandy to England and saw Margaret's mother talking to Margaret's nurse."[29] But it was not always a time of triumph, as one man recalled: "on the following night he was taken by the Scots and led away to Scotland, where he stayed for the next six weeks," or he "was taken prisoner in Brittany in the following year and held to ransom," or he "had a brother John killed by Welsh robbers at Hargrave on that day," or he had been "injured in the head and shin at the Battle of Shrewsbury."[30] Life near the borders carried dangers, as we learn from the man who recalled that "on that day [he] was captured by the Scots enemy and taken into Scotland," or another poor fellow who "knew because he was wounded on the day of the birth at a great battle between the Scots and the English at Carlisle."[31] Nor was life near the coast always much safer: the juror "knows because on the same day Bretons entered Ilfracombe and there took two men and set out to sea with them and nearly took a ship [of the juror himself]."[32]

Some of these memories were not as personal, nor as painful, and they allow us to see how the affairs of the great and mighty not only touched lesser folk but were remembered. Without claiming any role for himself, one juror offered that "the year before Richard's birth there was a battle at Shrewsbury and on 22 July last 22 years had passed since this battle."[33] Perhaps it was better just to be a spectator, as with the man who had seen "Henry, Prince of Wales, first born of Henry IV, ride with a great army through Little Dewchurch. The prince was on his way from Hereford to Monmouth, and on 30 November last 21 years had passed since then."

This was a better brush with Glendower's rebellion than was recounted by the juror who said that "on that day Owyn Glendordy came with his large army to the gates of Cardiff," or by another poor fellow "who was taken by Welsh rebels at Cat's Ash near Ragiet and plundered of all his belongings."[34] It was an up-and-down matter, for in the same Proof we have a memory of when "the village of Chanstone was burnt and destroyed by a sudden invasion of the Welsh rebels on the day of the baptism," and—from a fellow juror—a memory "that Richard Lord Grey of Codnor, rode with his army through Poston to the Castle of Grosmont to resist the Welsh rebels."[35]

Sometimes the relevant memory was simply a way of dating, another of those coincidental overlaps that helped mark the time of birth and baptism. Two jurors told of "that day [on which] the King's French enemies burnt Portsmouth near Drayton and the king's bailiff warned them to be ready to resist."[36] No indication of any personal involvement by the juror who recalled that "on that day a ship from foreign parts was wrecked in a great storm and broke into pieces on the sea coast of Hutton. One part of it was taken possession of by the king's ministers of his duchy of Lancaster."[37] Given what still resonates from the past, we note the single memory that points out that "Edward was born in the year after the rebellion of the commons of England ... which was in the summer 22 years ago."[38] It was hard to take in much more of the outside world than with the joint memory of five men at Warwick, they saying "that Roger was 23 because it was commonly said at Coventry at Corpus Christi [19 May] that the wife of John Deyncourt had borne a son, Roger, at Whitsun in the castle. A certain Roger Beauford, brother of the pope [Gregory XI], a prisoner of John duke of Lancaster in the custody of John Deyncourt in the castle, was his godfather."[39]

There are more of these memories: men wounded, men going off to war, people suffering when a French ship landed to wreak havoc. In the same realm, in the same culture, people had common experiences and to some degree, common memories about them. There might be an old soldier's tale—probably another of those oft-told memories: "Richard Maynard, 54, was with the duke of Lancaster in Spain at that time and when he returned home was told that Nicholas was then aged one year, and seeing him judged that that was correct."[40] At least one memory rings down a happier note on martial memories, as one man recalled that he "knows because the day of truces between England and Scotland was held at Hawden Stank on 3 November following."[41]

As our escheators asked at the start, "how do you remember," at least the material we have seen here would be likely to leave a lasting memory. Moreover, much of it was common memory—social lore—and a question we ask is why there were not more joint memories of memorable, external events. How often did the king ride by, we may well ask? When we looked at memories of baptism, why was it only one juror of 12 who talked of having seen Henry V lift the infant from the font? How often did the earl of Northumberland come to the village on a recruiting drive? Some jurors chose to tell of such seemingly memorable events, even while most of their fellows turned to the familiar tales of births and marriages and deaths—universals—whereas men at arms, and even French and Scottish raiders, come and go.

NOTES

1. In the next chapter we note several memories of "miracle cures" that took place at English sites.
2. 20/844: In the second memory (17/429) the jurors had only come from as far away as Bedford, so it was hardly a grand tour.
3. 19/782. This is the only pilgrimage memory that tells of a journey to two of the three major centers. Usually one holy site seems to have sufficed.
4. 25/127. The juror-pilgrim spoke at a Proof at Dorchester, Oxfordshire, so his journey was not a long one.
5. 16/947: 15/449.
6. 15/159: 19/999.
7. 18/1180: 19/1002.
8. 23/602.
9. 18/311. This seems to indicate both the monastic vows and ordination (22/677).
10. 15/450: 16/947.
11. 15/159: 22/827.
12. 15/660.
13. 25/127.
14. 19/785: 22/228. There was also a son who became a Franciscan at the house in York (15/893).
15. 15/893.
16. 23/419, with the relationship to the juror indicated by the names, rather than explicitly: 21/871, and for a similar brother-in-law memory, 21/876. Some of our jurors were of the social level that produced men who rose to high monastic office.
17. 23/422.

18. 24/721.
19. 20/846. It seems likely that the juror's name—Bagshoth—and that of the late prioress—Bongesett—indicate a kinship link.
20. 25/351: 15/291.
21. For a comparison, in the index of Vol. 16 of the *Inquisitions Post Mortem,* under "occupations," the following are listed: apothecary, arblaster, brewer, butcher, cornchandler, draper, grocer, hurrer ("hurar"), maltmonger, ropemaker, "sherman" skinner, surgeon, vintner, waxchandler, and weaver.
22. 22/677.
23. 23/596.
24. 24/126.
25. 23/139.
26. 22/839.
27. 26/468.
28. 18/953.
29. 23/415. The heiress was 14 and the Proof was held on 2 December 1429.
30. 15/275: 19/392: 19/1001: 22/529.
31. 19/791: 23: 314.
32. 26/143.
33. 22/529.
34. 23/140: 20/184: 23/417.
35. 23/598.
36. 19/1002.
37. 24/721. This was a Lincolnshire Proof from 1436.
38. 18/854. The proof was taken on 27 May 1403 for an heir born on 21 May 1382.
39. 18/311.
40. 19/392. The Proof was held in 1408, regarding a birth in 1387. Visual evidence of the heir's age was frequently cited in early Proofs but rarely seems of much importance by the time of Richard II (Vol.15 of the *Inquisitions*).
41. 25/295. The Proof was from 1438 and 1417, would have been the year of "the truces."

CHAPTER 7

Memory Is a Strange Country

Abstract When the 12 memories of a Proof of Age are read as a single document, they usually focus on a few familiar themes and it is easy to see how the jurors shared a common village life. In a few Proofs there was even a "theme" that covered at least half the memories: a gift for the mother at her churching, the death of valuable animals, and so on. In many Proofs there were joint memories: four men said as one that they had seen the priest write the date of the baptism, and many more statements of this sort. But there were some odd memories and we wonder that only one juror went back to that event: a comet, the burning of a Lollard, deaths from the plague. So in aggregate the hundreds of Proofs attest to the common threads that run through lives that share culture and class (and gender) and they also provide an occasional glimpse into a few once-and-only events that were offered as a memory to mark the year under consideration.

Keywords Collectivve memory • Memorable events

Like the past, memory is a strange country. In our efforts to reconstruct the run of life—private and family, in the village and beyond, the routine and the unusual—we have worked from the idea that the memories of roughly common and similar life experience are oft-times reflected in the

J.T. Rosenthal, *Social Memory in Late Medieval England*, The New Middle Ages, https://doi.org/10.1007/978-3-319-69700-0_7

mnemonics of the thousands of jurors whose brief statements we have organized and analyzed. Moreover, we have worked from the idea—well supported by most of the memories—that there was little change in ordinary life between the 1370s and the 1440s, at least as reported in the Proofs. Day in and day out, things were much the same, though kings might come and go and wars be won and lost (mostly lost). Moreover, while the nature of an administrative-cum-legal proceeding would serve to reinforce this conservative aspect of the Proofs, it was primarily the basic sameness of life and experience that was the main reason for the static or stable nature of the jurors' world as reflected in most of their memories.

In looking to organize and categorize the jurors' memories we had no problem in setting up some large and inclusive categories: being at the baptism, fetching the wet-nurse, remembering a death in the family, a business arrangement preserved in a document, a fire in the village, a broken shin, a dead horse, and more of such. Given the sameness of life experience and of the Proofs' memories, it may not seem a great stretch to picture the escheator, or perhaps that first juror who was often a sort of *de facto* foreman or village headman, turning to the others and offering a suggestion about the sort of event that would jog their memory. Who among them, the escheator might enquire, could offer a reasonably specific memory of the heir's baptism, even if only as a spectator, or who among them could offer a life-cycle event in his own family around that critical time, or who had gone on a pilgrimage that year, or who had helped fight a fire, and more of this kind of categorization. Mostly the responses came in the form of individualized memories of such events and milestones, though a fair number—as we have seen—were offered as joint memories, the common statement of two or more men speaking in unison about a joint experience that had left the legacy of a joint memory.

But against the flow of the current, a few memories stand out against the run of normal life events, out of the vast numbers of memories focused on baptism or marriage. These are not only striking memories, but they raise the question of why only one juror chose that "out-of-the-loop" event as his key memory. What these odd memories tell us is that, while we mostly "go with the flow," there is the chance that one man pegged a given year, and his recollection of that year, on something of a special nature that remained as *the* memory for him, though not for any of his fellows. Each man's memory bank was his own, to dip into as he chose, and these oddly eccentric or individualized memories put flesh on the bones of our generalization, few though they are.

In constructing our mosaic of memory and life as revealed in bits and pieces that we have been assembling, we have mostly been concerned to focus on the common themes and topics that run in considerable numbers through the 12 volumes of *Inquisitions*. Now, for a final look at our jurors' memories, we look at the odd memories that were offered but once. They, in a sense, go against the flow. But first, to sharpen the contrast, we will think of a few inquisitions as a single document and tally the kinds of memories that go to make up the whole package (of 12). If we look at a Proof from the 1380s, and one without any indication of any great drama or memories of the anomalous or the outré, we find that conventional memories about mainstream events set the tone.[1] The 12 memories are "the usual suspects," telling of the death of the juror's wife, the birth of a son, the death of a grandmother, the birth of twin sons, the death of a son "whom he loved to hold," a juror's marriage, the birth of a son, the attestation of that godfather for whom the baby was named, the death of an uncle, the birth of a son, the birth of a daughter, and the death of a brother, "killed at Easter." What is a bit unusual here but seemingly without any larger significance is that each memory is framed in terms of the ecclesiastical calendar: "Sunday after Annunciation next," or "on the Feast of the nativity of St John the Baptist," or "the Ash Wednesday after." To classify the memories, six of the twelve relate to a birth affecting the juror, one to a marriage, and four to a death. All the memories stayed close to home, all within the community and culture of the village. Some are personal if hardly intimate; others are just separate contributions to the common life of the community. They mostly reflect the roll-over of the generations.

If we jump ahead by a half-century and look at a Proof from 1433, we see a wider divergence, though this is a chance dip, not an argument for any change over time in either village life or social memory.[2] Here the memories tell us of the death of wife, a son's birth, a building consumed by fire, the acquisition of a tenement, a fall from a horse resulting in a broken right shin (incurred while the juror was on his way to speak with the father), the payment of £20 to get quittance of a debt, a marriage, having the date of the birth entered into a missal, a daughter's marriage, the rendering of an account (with the juror having been jailed because he was in arrears), witnessing the baptism and drinking wine afterward, and having a ship sunk. Still in the village, though with some memories looking more to personal or individual activities and without that heavy focus on the birth-marriage-death trio that pretty much took over the first Proof.

But that is just the luck of the draw—the particular Proof that we chose for this exposition. Presumably in the latter case each juror would have known the substance of the other men's memories: familiar events and some with a public or community face. However, the memories were all personal in that they did not affect any of the others. Rather, each one reflected each juror's choice of what to offer and it just happened that in the Proof each man came up with something that did not seem to affect or involve his fellows, except in so far as they had been neighbors and co-residents of the village.

This seems to be a pattern for many of the Proofs, though after one more analysis of this sort we move on to some memories with more exotic or dramatic information. A Yorkshire Proof from 1434 follows much in the footsteps of the two previous ones.[3] Here we do get some memories of life-milestone events about others, that is, memories of people not of the family of the juror or the heir. The 12 memories tell us of a woman who had had fraternal twins, of the juror's own marriage, of the death of a juror's son, of the birth of a son, of the juror's presentation of salmon and pike to the heir's father, of the juror who carried a torch to the church, of the juror who carried two pots of wine for the godparents, of the man sent to York to fetch the wet-nurse, of the churching of the juror's wife, of the juror's son who carried a basin and ewer to church, of the birth of a son (now aged 21 and more), and of the marriage of some other party. This gives us four birth-related memories (including the churching), two looking at marriage, and only one account of a death (and we are told that it came after a long illness). Some of the 12 men here had been more active in the theater of baptism, though supporting roles were their level of involvement, while the other memories were much in the networks of family and village lore. Not much beyond these boundaries, except perhaps the trip to York and even that was part of the routines of birth and baptism.

By way of contrast with this heavy focus on the usual themes that are the bread and butter of almost all the Proofs, we can turn to the Proofs wherein we have at least one memory that deviated sharply from the standard lines of recollection: the occasional splash of bright color that stands out against the general patterns of the many. What is particularly striking in these Proofs is the way that one man's memory of the unusual event was almost never the memory offered by his fellows, though the other jurors were presumably men who also had been exposed to whatever it was that their fellow juror chose to talk about.

In a few Proofs a juror—and it almost always was just one of the twelve—offers a memory that points us toward what we can think of as the moral economy of the village. These would seem to be outstanding memories: the sort of memory of "yes, it was in that year that...," even if only offered by one of the twelve. Furthermore, as some of these memories were about sexual behavior, it is surprising that only one juror (or in rare joint memory of three men), pulled these tales out of the memory-storehouse. Three men, in a common testimony, did say they "know because on the same day a certain priest called Sir John Launcy went round the church by way of penance with a women called Joan Wynkman and they saw it."[4] In this case it was both the man and the woman who were fingered, while in other such memories—and there are but very few—more blame fell on *her* than on *him*. One juror remembered when "John Homn-e ... town bailiff placed Alice Blast on the tumbril in the vill, called 'a Gumscole,' for many defaults and transgressions perpetrated by her to the harm of the whole vill of Kidderminster."[5] We know who got the sharp end of the stick in the recollection of when "Margaret Morey of Loddon was then pregnant by Thomas Holme, chaplain, and for shame took her goods on the following morning and left the town."[6] Less obvious and perhaps not as salacious is the memory offered by one juror who had "prosecuted a cause of defamation against John Gavelok, with the result that John went naked around the churchyard ... solemnly for three days with a burning candle in his hand. Thomas [the juror] recollected that John observed this penance for three Sundays after Gerard's birth."[7] There may have been a tale of infidelity and cuckolding in the cryptic memory of a juror who spoke of his own experience: "on the same day his wife Lettice beat him for which her neighbours ... carried Richard Fox, her nearest neighbour, to the water according to the custom of the country (*secumdum modum patrie*)."[8] Sometimes it was a small event: the juror "knows because Alice Bradepole ran away from her master."[9] Elusive and allusive: the memory of a juror who "with others performed a great play in the vill ... to which Gerard [the baby] was carried by his nurse."[10]

We offered a few references to deaths caused by the plague. Given the nature of the disease—familiar, deadly, much-discussed, widespread—that only a bare handful of memories talk of its presence also seems peculiar, though perhaps it was an ill omen to speak of it.[11] But some other breaks in the routine were likely to be in the one-time-only category, though it was just a single juror, on each occasion, who used strange phenomena as his point of recollection. One man recalled that the baby's mother "spoke with him on the day of her churching after Richard's birth ... about a comet that shone the preceding year [*stella comata que fulgebat*] which was 22 years ago."[12] Another "act of God" memory was of the time when "there was an earthquake through all England when [the baby] was born in May 21 years ago"[13] At least the man who told of strange events at Pontefract seems to have been there on his own: "there [he] saw a man unknown to him who had been arrested for casting the evil eye on the horse of his neighbor"[14] though maybe he was not with his village cronies at the time (though we can be certain it would have been be a familiar tale by the time he offered it at the Proof).

In the thousands of jurors' memories that we have worked with, almost all were well-grounded in the world. Despite the countless references to the parish church, to various rituals, to the ecclesiastical calendar, and to the men and women of the church, jurors stuck to things one could see, hear, taste (on occasion), and touch. Only two memories move us into the world beyond the senses. One memory was a terse account of a miracle cure. Our juror, now aged 44, says that he "fell from his cart and broke his right leg. His friends carried him to Salisbury and placed him before the tomb of St. Osmond in the chapel of St. Mary in the cathedral church. He was then miraculously healed."[15] This was impressive, though a comparable memory from the North was going to top this, as we learn from a juror who had a somewhat longer memory to relate: "the translation of St. William is celebrated on 8 June in the province of York, and on the day of William Ingilby's birth [the heir] a miracle took place after the prayers and divine service in honour of St. William. One of Richard's boys called Wilfrid was exhausted by fever to the point of death but he was saved by St. William on that day."[16]

A few more memories of events that were not likely to be repeated and, whatever revived these particular memories, were not apt to be forgotten. Two references to heresy—a new disease in the realm and one to be treated accordingly. At a Proof held in Southwark in 1432, "Roger Poynt, 50 and more, agrees with John Brown. A heretic was burnt at Smithfield."[17] Pretty bald and no indication of whether the juror had been a witness or just knew of this from hearsay. And to conclude this look at the peculiar memories that belonged to just one man, we have a more circumstantial memory of the Lollards. At a Proof held at Brentwood in Essex on 29 October 1435 and talking about a baptism of 31 October 1413 ("22 years have passed since then") our singular juror has much to say. "John Kempe, 63 and more, says that on the day and year abovesaid, at Horndon on the

Hill, many Lollards gathered with insurgents against the church's power and privilege and, like disturbers, destroyed the king's peace, proposing that the young be not baptised, to the prejudice, destruction and scorn of the entire church. Thomas Malgrave [the father] ... afraid that Richard [the baby] would be killed unbaptized, ordered many armed men, of whom he [the juror]was one, for defense and to destroy the force and their diabolic intention. They fought the Lollards on the same evening ... and two hundred of them were thrown to the ground and killed. Richard was born and baptised on the same day and this battle happened twenty-two years ago."[18]

What did John Kempe's fellow jurors have to offer when their turn came? Nothing along these lines, as we have come to expect. The other jurors' memories ran in the familiar channels. The first juror at that Proof had been "seised in demesne as of fee of a messuage in Hornden and then had lost two horses and two cows when a stable collapsed." In fairness, these were fairly significant points in the juror's life, whatever he knew about the events at Horndon. He was followed by a man who said his servant had had his shin broken when a bear broke loose from a bear-baiting. Then came men who told of having purchased a messuage, of having purchased 20 quarters of malt (and who had two cart horses die when the load collapsed), one who had had 40 stolen sheep drown and the manor of Drayton burn, and one who had lost 12 sheep. Their fellows told of the coroner's viewing of the body of a man who had been blown into the Thames. More familiar memories: the confirmation of a daughter, a fire, a broken shin and arm, and a fall while chasing a felon. These are events the memory of which might well remain vivid and, collectively, they give us one of those theme-Proofs, this time touching the loss of animals and injuries to humans, both to the jurors and to others. But only John Kempe, telling of a pitched battle with the Lollards, had a tale for the larger history of the realm.[19]

So the conclusion is that memory is both our link to a social identity—what we shared with others—and a key to our separate, individualized existence. Why did no one else of the other 11 men at Brentwood on that day look back to October 1413, and tell of a pitched battle against those who would show "scorn of the entire church"? But we can also ask why no one but those solitary jurors we mentioned above tell of an earthquake or a comet. Even a common experience that seemed divorced from the give-and-take of village life seemingly passed into the shadows of the un-remembered, as with the single reference to "remember because at that time [1377] all persons of both sexes, aged 14 and more, had to pay the king 4d."[20] It is a bit late to ask the escheator to push for more details or for corroboration of those "out of the loop" memories. Were we to be summoned today to tell our tales at a Proof in this day and age, we would probably not be in great accord in fixing one singular event looking back to 1996. Nor, along this same line, are we likely to have much better luck in lining up our 12 good men and true for common memories if we push along to the year 2038, when asked "How do you remember about 2017?" A question yet to be answered.

NOTES

1. 16/81. The Proof for John de Dalton, son and heir of John Dalton, knight, and held at Lancaster on 1 February, 7 Richard II.
2. 24/124. the Proof is of Elizabeth, daughter of William Bykebury and Joan his wife, and it was held at Modbury Devon, in June 1433.
3. 24/274. Proof of Brian de Stapilton, son of Brian de Stapilton, chevalier, and Proof held on 4 February 1434.
4. 16/341.
5. 22/673.
6. 19/783.
7. 22/827.
8. 17/148.
9. 25/526.
10. 22/827.
11. 23/413: 23/417.
12. 22/529.
13. 18/854. This is the Proof in which one juror—and only one—refers to the "rebellion of the commons."
14. 18/854.
15. 22/828.
16. 23/309.
17. 23/718.
18. 24/566.
19. 24/566.
20. 20/842. A joint memory from two men, one being 62, the other 65.

BIBLIOGRAPHY

SELECT BIBLIOGRAPHY

Bailey, B. Gregory. "Coming of Age and Family in Medieval England." *Journal of Family History* 33, no. 2 (2008): 41–60.

Bedell, J. "Memory and Proof of Age in England, 1272–1327." *Past & Present* 162 (1999): 3–27.

Britton, C.I. *A Meteorological Chronology to A.D. 1450*, Meteorological Office, Geophysical Memoirs, no. 70, 136–77. HMSO: London, 1937.

Chew, Helena M. "The Office of Escheator in the City of London During the Middle Ages." *English Historical Review* 58 (1943): 319–30.

Clanchy, M.T. *From Memory to Written Record: England 1066–1307*, 2nd ed. Oxford: Blackwell, 1993.

Connerton, Paul. *How Societies Remember.* Cambridge: Cambridge University Press, 1989.

Deller, W.D. "The Texture of Literacy in the Memories of Late Medieval Proof-of-Age Jurors." *Journal of Medieval History* 38, no. 2 (2012): 1–15.

———. "Proof of Age 1246 to 1430: Their Nature, Veracity and Use as Sources." In *The Later Medieval Inquisitions Post Mortem: Mapping the Medieval Countryside and Rural Society*, ed. Michael Hicks, 136–60. Woodbridge: Boydell, 2016.

Donahue, Charles, Jr. "Proof by Witnesses in the Church Courts of Medieval England: An Imperfect Reception of Learned Law." In *On the Laws and Customs of England: Essays in Honor of Samuel E. Thorne*, ed. Morris S. Arnold, et al., 127–58. Charlotte, NC: University of North Caroline Press, 1981.

Fentress, James, and Chris Wickham. *Social Memory.* Oxford: Blackwell, 1992.

© The Author(s) 2018

J.T. Rosenthal, *Social Memory in Late Medieval England*, The New Middle Ages, https://doi.org/10.1007/978-3-319-69700-0

Gillett, E. "Proofs of Age." *The Amateur Historian* 5, no. 1961–63 (1962): 224–30.

Harris-Stoertz, Fione. "Remembering Birth in the Thirteenth and Fourteenth Century." In *Reconsidering Gender: Time and Memory in Medieval Culture,* ed. Elizabeth Cox, et al., 25–59. Rochester, NY: D. S. Brewer, 2015.

———. "Midwives in the Middle Ages: Birth Attendants." In *Medicine and the Law in the Middle Ages,* ed. Wendy J. Turner, et al., 58–87. Turnhout: Brepols, n.d.

Holford, Matthew. "'Testimony (to Some Extent Fictitious):' Proofs of Age in the First Half of the Fifteenth Century." *Historical Research* 82 (2008): 1–25.

———, ed. *Calendar of Inquisitions Post Mortem, Vol. xxvi (21–25 Henry VI) (1442–47)*. London/Woodbridge: National Archives/Boydell, 2009.

Holford, Matthew, S.A. Mileson, C.B. Noble, and Kate Parkin, eds. *Calendar of Inquisitions Post Mortem, Vol. xxiv (11–15 Henry VI) (1432–37)*. London/Woodbridge: National Archives/Boydell, 2010.

Kirby, J.L., ed. *Calendar of Inquisitions Post Mortem, Vol. xv (1–7 Richard II)*. London: HMSO, 1970.

———., ed. *Calendar of Inquisitions Post Mortem, Vol. xvi (7–15 Richard II)*. London: HMSO, 1974.

———., ed. *Calendar of Inquisitions Post Mortem, Vol. xviii (1–6 Henry IV) (1399–1405)*. London: HMSO, 1987.

———., ed. *Calendar of Inquisitions Post Mortem, Vol. xvii (15–23 Richard II)*. London: HMSO, 1988.

———., ed. *Calendar of Inquisitions Post Mortem, Vol. xix (7–14 Henry IV) (1405–1413)*. London: HMSO, 1992.

———., ed. *Calendar of Inquisitions Post Mortem, Vol. xx (1–5 Henry V) (1413–1418)*. London: HMSO, 1995.

Kirby, J.L., and Janet A. Stevenson, eds. *Calendar of Inquisitions Post Mortem, Vol. xxi (6–10 Henry V)*. London/Woodbridge: Public Record Office/Boydell, 2002.

Lynch, Joseph H. *Godparents and Kinship in Early Medieval Europe*. Princeton: Princeton University Press, 1986.

McGlynne, Margaret. "Memory, Orality, and Life Records: Proofs of Age in Tudor England." *Sixteenth Century Journal* 40, no. 3 (2009): 679–97.

Murray, Alexander. *Suicide in the Middle Ages*. Oxford: Oxford University Press, 1998.

Noble, Claire, ed. *Calendar of Inquisitions Post Mortem, Vol. xxiii (6–10 Henry VI) (1427–1432)*. London/Woodbridge: National Archives/Boydell, 2004.

———, ed. *Calendar of Inquisitions Post Mortem, Vol. xxv (16–20 Henry VI) (1437–1442)*. London/Woodbridge: National Archives/Boydell, 2009.

Parkin, Kate, ed. *Calendar of Inquisitions Post Mortem, Vol. 22 (1–5 Henry VI) (1422–27)*. London/Woodbridge: National Archives and Public Record Office/Boydell, 2003.

Rosenthal, Joel T. *Telling Tales: Sources and Narration in Late Medieval England*. University Park, PA: Pennsylvania State University Press, 2003.

Smith, L. Beverley. "Proof of Age in Medieval Wales." *Bulletin of the Board of Celtic Studies* 38 (1991): 134–44.

Stevenson, E.R. "The Escheator." In *The English Government at Work: II – Fiscal Administration*, ed. W.A. Morris and Joseph R. Strayer, 109–67. Cambridge, MA: The Medieval Academy, 1947.

Thomas, Keith. "Numeracy in Early Modern England." *Transactions of the Royal Historical Society*, 5th Series 37 (1987): 103–32.

Walker, Sue Sheridan. "Proof of Age of Heirs in Medieval England." *Mediaeval Studies* 35 (1973): 306–23.

INDEX[1]

[1] Note: Page numbers followed by 'n' refers to notes.

© The Author(s) 2018
J.T. Rosenthal, *Social Memory in Late Medieval England*, The New Middle Ages, https://doi.org/10.1007/978-3-319-69700-0